*American Secondary Schools*

# THE PROFESSIONAL EDUCATION FOR TEACHERS SERIES

*Under the Editorship of* PAUL WOODRING

*Editor of the Educational Supplement of the* Saturday Review,
*and Distinguished Service Professor at Western Washington State College*

**PUBLISHED TITLES**

*Introduction to American Education,* Paul Woodring

*Education and Democratic Ideals,* Gordon C. Lee

*Education in Western Culture,* Robert Ulich

*American Secondary Schools,* Mauritz Johnson, Jr.

Volumes on the following topics are in preparation: Elementary Education, Innovations in Education, Human Growth and Development, Learning in the Schools, Measurement and Evaluation, Social Psychology in Education.

# American

# Secondary Schools

## MAURITZ JOHNSON, Jr.
*Cornell University*

*Harcourt, Brace & World, Inc.*
*New York · Chicago · Burlingame*

Library of Congress Catalog Card Number: 65-26741

Printed in the United States of America

# Editor's Foreword

The term "secondary education" does not lend itself to precise definition. Over the years it has been applied to a wide variety of institutions which have little in common except that all carry education beyond the elementary level and stop short of the university level. But public high schools, the predominant American secondary schools of the twentieth century, are well known to the college students who will read this book, most of whom have attended either four-year high schools or junior and senior high schools and have viewed them through a student's eyes.

The prospective teacher can build upon the knowledge of these institutions he gained as a student. But he should recognize that American secondary education is undergoing continuous change which, in some parts of the nation, is so rapid and dramatic that the schools in which he will teach will differ substantially from those he attended only a few years ago. This book will help him to understand the nature of institutional change and the need for it and to prepare himself for the innovations that will come during his professional lifetime.

Although certification practices in most states distinguish secondary from elementary teachers, the differences in professional preparation are much smaller than they were a generation ago or even a decade ago. Most of the professional courses now required for certification can be made appropriate for teachers at both levels. But, at some point in the professional sequence, it is necessary for the prospective secondary teacher to focus his attention sharply on the specific institution in which he plans to teach. This volume provides such a focus. It may be used, depending on the sequence of required courses, as the basis for a course in secondary education or —in MAT and similar programs—in a seminar that accompanies the internship.

In writing this book, Professor Johnson has drawn upon more

than twenty years of professional experience as a high-school teacher and principal, director of experimental projects in secondary education, and professor of secondary education. His writing reveals a wide familiarity not only with the professional literature but with innovations that have not yet become a part of the literature. He has a firm knowledge of the present and the past but his eye is on the future. His purpose is to help prepare better teachers for the schools of tomorrow.

PAUL WOODRING

# *Preface*

This book is addressed to prospective secondary-school teachers. In it I discuss some matters I believe teachers should know and think about before they enter upon their chosen work. Reading it will make no one a more skillful teacher. All that the reader can hope for is to increase somewhat his understanding of American secondary education as it has been, now is, and could be. With a better understanding of the institution he serves, the teacher may be able to serve it more effectively.

Having experienced secondary education himself, the reader already knows much about the subject. And being intelligent, he undoubtedly has formed conclusions regarding needed improvements. Still, he may have had direct experience with no more than one or two schools; he may not have been aware of the rationale underlying much of what went on around him; and having been personally involved and somewhat immature at the time, he may have taken for granted much that he is now in a better position to examine critically. This volume may help him carry out such a critical examination.

Teachers must recognize the crucial role they play in all attempts to improve secondary education. Without their endorsement and participation, no one else can effect changes of any consequence in the schools. Nor can anyone long resist their insistent demands for change. Secondary-school teachers are individually responsible for their performance in teaching their subjects. But in addition they are collectively responsible for the quality of secondary education as a whole in their schools. They cannot, therefore, disclaim interest in and concern about those problems of secondary education which transcend their own fields. Indeed, they must arrive at, and be prepared to articulate, their own positions on a variety of questions.

I have tried to make my own positions clear in this book. I make no secret of my bias in favor of a stronger intellectual emphasis than has prevailed in most secondary schools. The reader is free to disagree with me. Alternative views are indicated. Some writers on secondary education attempt to take a "neutral" stand. They give readers the impression that, since all practices have their advantages and disadvantages, it is a matter of indifference which are adopted. Most writers who try to be "objective" fail, however, and actually, though perhaps unwittingly, espouse the prevailing orthodoxy.

What is orthodox is by no means all bad. Many established practices in secondary schools are worthy of being retained. Obviously, much of value and validity has been learned from many years of experience in devising a system of universal secondary education. But no policy or practice should be exempt from careful re-examination. He who would criticize must first, however, inform himself.

This brief volume provides no more than an overview of secondary education. It contains no statistical tables, charts, or graphs, no pictures or diagrams, and no lists of any kind. I am well aware that many topics which might have been included were not and that many which were included could have been developed more fully. But this book is not intended for specialists in secondary education. It will have served its purpose if it provokes thought, provides a basis for discussion, and encourages prospective teachers to investigate some topics further in the suggested readings.

Exciting possibilities lie ahead for secondary education in the last third of this century. Scholarly teachers with strong commitments to the ideals of both quality and equality can, if they persevere and dare, create a system of secondary education that will link each community in the nation with that universal community of scholars which is dedicated to the advancement of man's knowledge and the preservation of mankind's noblest achievements.

MAURITZ JOHNSON, JR.

# Contents

# Chapter One

# Goals and Functions

Never before and nowhere else has universal secondary education been so nearly achieved as in the United States today. Over 90 per cent of all young people between 14 and 17 years of age are in school. Two out of three of the more than 15 million students enrolled in secondary schools will graduate. More than 40 per cent of the country's adult population are high-school graduates.

The secondary school serves as a source of leaders for the nation and as an avenue to opportunity for the individual. And as a college degree becomes more and more a requisite for both leadership and opportunity, secondary education is more essential than ever. For all its unparalleled accomplishments, however, the American secondary school continues to be faced with formidable problems related to quantity, quality, and equality. If its teachers are to help solve these problems, they must be well informed about the institution itself.

The phrase "the American secondary school" suggests that the United States has a unified system of education consisting of a number of more or less similar individual schools. Actually, there are over fifty separate state and territorial systems, in which roughly 30,000 educational institutions at the precollegiate level serve students who have completed their elementary education. These secondary schools differ so greatly in their support, control, size, comprehensiveness, clientele, and quality that it is difficult, and often deceptive, to generalize about them. Almost anything one chooses to say about them will prove to be true of some, but not of others.

On some matters, of course, statistics reveal the situation that exists in the majority of secondary schools, but only on a limited number of features are data available for all schools. It is possible to know a great deal about one particular school, or even several, and yet no one can know everything about even a single school. Still, the temptation is strong to make all kinds of assertions purporting to represent "most American secondary schools," despite the lack of ac-

tual evidence to support such statements. Indeed, it would be difficult to document many of the generalizations made in this book.

Even documented information regarding "most schools" is often
misinterpreted. One common error is equating what is prevalent
with what is desirable. Most American schools do not offer instruction in the Russian language, but this may not be a desirable state of
affairs. The trend is probably toward increased offerings in Russian.
But trends are not necessarily desirable either. A trend may merely
represent a fad, or it may be a sign of retrogression or error and thus
better resisted than followed.

A second error in dealing with statistics about American secondary schools is confusing numbers of schools with numbers of students. A large number of very small schools serve a relatively small
proportion of the students in the country. Therefore, what may be
true of most of the *schools* may not affect most of the *students*. And
it is what happens to students that is of greatest significance in any
discussion of education.

What actually happens to students in a school depends on many
factors. Schools are organized institutions in which the desired seldom happens unless it is deliberately planned to happen. If certain
experiences are not offered, certain results do not ensue. If a school
is to offer particular experiences, it must provide appropriate facilities, adequate time, and qualified teachers. Even then, it must undertake careful evaluation to determine whether the desired results
were achieved.

All this planning, staffing, scheduling, evaluating and supplying
of facilities calls for efficient organization and skillful administration. But the sole purpose of administration is to make possible effective teaching, which in turn seeks to ensure that students have the
kinds of experience that result in the desired learning. Basic, therefore, to both administration and teaching is agreement on what
results are desired and attainable. In a system of nearly universal
secondary education it is not easy to reach agreement on the goals to
be sought and the functions to be served.

## PAST PURPOSES

The contemporary American, who takes universal, free, public secondary education for granted, needs to be reminded how very recently such a system of education came into being. Ancient Greece in
all its grandeur and Rome in its glory educated only men, not

women, and only freemen at that, not slaves. During the Middle Ages future clerics received an education, but few of the laity did; during the Renaissance an education was accorded to future courtiers but rarely to the common people. Throughout most of history the ruled masses either were provided with no education at all or with a different kind of education from that given to the ruling classes.

In this country the distinction persisted in the existence of two parallel forms of education which differed in duration, in the subjects taught, and even in the language used for instruction. The colonists of New England set up reading and writing schools for the majority of their children, but children who were destined to be leaders of the church, and hence of the government, attended Latin grammar schools that offered instruction in Latin and Greek. In a sense, the Boston Latin Grammar School, which opened in 1635, was the first American secondary school, but, since it did not follow but rather paralleled the "primary" school of the day, it was a "secondary" school only in that it offered precollegiate education.

With the founding of the United States, the ruled became the rulers, and the story since then has been one of more and more education for more and more people. During the early years of the nineteenth century, virtually every crossroads settlement established "common schools" to provide the children of the "common people" with a basic elementary education. Before compulsory attendance laws were passed, many children attended the common school for only a few years and for only a few months each year. But both the length and number of terms attended increased steadily. At the secondary level, private academies superseded the exclusive Latin grammar schools. These academies offered both college-preparatory work and practical studies to middle-class boys and, for the first time, to their sisters as well.

Although Benjamin Franklin founded an academy in Philadelphia in 1751, that institution soon became a college and, later, the University of Pennsylvania. So we can say that the true beginning of the academy movement was the founding of the Phillips Academies in New England during the Revolution. Academies flourished throughout the first half of the nineteenth century, not only in New England but in New York, where they received public aid, and in the new states of the Northwest Territory. The early academies accepted young pupils who had not completed the common-school program. As public common schools became common in number as well as in name, however, the academies gradually became true "secondary" schools and admitted only elementary-school graduates. Although they offered a number of practical subjects, and although relatively few of their graduates entered college, the academies of the nineteenth century gave more and more emphasis to college-preparatory courses.

The private academy had its period of greatest growth in the decade beginning in 1825, though an event in 1821 had already foreshadowed its ultimate decline. In that year, again in Boston, the first public "high school" appeared. Gradually other cities established high schools, and around 1850 several states permitted some common schools, by adding "academic" departments, to become union free schools. By 1875 there were more public high schools than academies in the nation. Some of the academies closed, some merged with high schools, some became normal schools or colleges, and some continued to exist as "prep" schools, perpetuating the tradition of private education. The legality of using tax money to support secondary schools did not go unquestioned. Finally, however, in 1873, Judge Cooley's famous ruling in the "Kalamazoo Case" declared such tax support constitutional and set the legal precedent that enabled the public high school to achieve its hegemony in American secondary education.

The nineteenth-century high school was in effect a public version of the academy. Like the academy, it was originally established to provide a practical education, but before long it, too, had begun to emphasize college-preparatory subjects. Though by 1875 high-school enrollments surpassed those of the academies, they were still relatively small. As late as 1893, when an eighth-grade education had become fairly common, an influential committee reported that the main function of the free public high school was ". . . to prepare for the duties of life that small proportion of all the children in the country who show themselves able to profit by an education prolonged to the eighteenth year, and whose parents are able to support them while they remain so long in school."[1]

&rarr; Between 1890 and 1930 the academic high school was transformed into a comprehensive school whose aim was to provide universal secondary education for "all American youth." Purposes and programs

[1] National Education Association, *Report of the Committee of Ten on Secondary School Studies*, American Book Co., 1893, pp. 56–57.

broadened while enrollments increased by a phenomenal 750 per cent, compared with a general population increase of only a little over 60 per cent. It is difficult to say to what extent enrollments increased because offerings became more attractive and to what extent offerings were altered to accommodate the changing clientele. The citizens of a mechanized, industrialized, urbanized America needed more education, but they needed an education that was different from what was being offered by the high school of 1900. Or so it seemed.

As the high-school program grew more comprehensive through the steady accretion of new subjects, the traditional academic subjects lost their position of dominance. Greek virtually disappeared, Latin waned, history became a part of social studies, relatively fewer students pursued advanced mathematics and science, and even the more recently introduced modern foreign languages declined in popularity. In 1906 the so-called Carnegie unit was made the standard measure of school credit. This development fostered the decline of academic studies by assigning equal credit to all subjects that were studied for equivalent lengths of time. When the federal government gave financial support to vocational courses through the Smith-Hughes Act of 1917, it indirectly promoted a further decline in the emphasis on academic subjects. Finally, with a 32-page report issued by the U.S. Bureau of Education in 1918,[2] came formal commitment to a new type of secondary education that subordinated intellectual development to other goals.

This report of a national commission on the reorganization of secondary education set forth seven objectives, of which only one explicitly, and then in a limited sense, referred to intellectual goals. In first and last positions on the list of objectives were two personal attributes—health and ethical character. Four objectives concerned preparation for various roles or activities in life—worthy home membership, citizenship, vocation, worthy use of leisure. Finally, representing still another dimension and appearing in second position in this mixed list was an objective called "command of the fundamental processes." These processes included such basic intellectual skills as reading, arithmetic, writing, and oral expression.

Although the publication of the cardinal principles was one of

[2] National Education Association, Commission on the Reorganization of Secondary Education, *Cardinal Principles of Secondary Education,* Bulletin 35, U.S. Bureau of Education, 1918.

the major events of this century in American secondary education, it probably affected practices less than it affected thinking. A number of subsequent statements regarding the objectives of secondary education either rephrased or amplified the seven objectives in the 1918 bulletin. The emphasis in these statements was on gross behavioral objectives—that is, on what students should be expected to *do* and on the roles in life in which they were expected to use what they learned. Thus one list included 43 items in four categories: self-realization, human relationship, civic responsibility, and economic efficiency.[3]

Another list identified the ten "imperative educational needs" of all American youth. These needs consisted of restated versions of the seven "cardinal" objectives, to which were added consumership, esthetic appreciation, and understanding of science. Significantly, the list began with "saleable skills"—the vocational objective—and relegated to last place the ability to think and to use language effectively.[4] Characteristically, however, no priority of needs was implied.

The omission or depreciation of traditional intellectual objectives in discussions of secondary education has been deplored by critics both outside and within the education profession. Some critics consider intellectual development the only legitimate objective of schools. Others recognize the need for broadening the purposes of secondary education but insist that intellectual goals should have priority. Support for the latter position came from the Educational Policies Commission in 1961 when it asserted that the central purpose of education was the cultivation of the ability to think.[5]

The strong emphasis on direct preparation for personal and civic roles in many of the earlier statements of objectives can probably be attributed in part, at least, to two influences—science and democracy. In 1859 Charles Darwin published his famous book, *On the Origin of Species*. A decade later, Herbert Spencer, the British scientific philosopher, applied the doctrine of evolution to education, advancing the idea that education should recognize natural priorities in equipping man for "complete living." As a scientist, he assigned top priority to activities that minister directly to self-preservation; then he listed activities related to earning a living, bearing and rearing chil-

[3] Educational Policies Commission, *Purposes of Education in American Democracy*, National Education Association, 1938.

[4] Educational Policies Commission, *Education for All American Youth*, National Education Association, 1944, pp. 225–26.

[5] Educational Policies Commission, *The Central Purpose of American Education*, National Education Association, 1961, p. 12.

dren, and participating in social and political life. The enjoyment of the refinements of culture he placed last.

The seven cardinal objectives clearly reflect Spencer's idea of education for complete living, and there were many subsequent efforts to aim secondary education explicitly at effective performance in various "persistent life situations."[6] The duty of the school was "to teach pupils to do better the desirable things they will do anyway."[7] What adults do in the course of living could be systematically analyzed in much the same way that a job analysis is made in industry. During the 1920's several efforts were made to analyze in remarkable detail the specific tasks people were called upon to perform in their various roles in life, on the assumption that the curriculum should directly prepare pupils for each task. The necessity for such direct preparation hinged on the rejection of "faculty psychology," with its formal discipline theory of transfer of training. This theory held that mental exercise strengthened memory, reason, imagination, and other mental faculties for general transfer to any situation in which they were needed. This view was rejected by many educators in favor of the more "scientific" psychological theory of E. L. Thorndike, which attributed transfer to the presence of identical elements in the learning and application situations. In short, "scientifically" derived objectives were to be met by a "scientifically" determined curriculum through a "scientifically" based methodology.

The ideal product of this scientific educative process was, in effect, the model "democratic citizen"—healthy, wealthy, and socially minded, if not wise. An intellectual orientation was construed as antithetical to democracy, for three reasons. First, such an orientation was traditionally associated with the education of the ruling classes and was therefore suspect for the masses, even though they now were ruling themselves. Second, because not all pupils were equally capable of pursuing intellectual learning, objectives more equally within the reach of all were deemed more consonant with the ideal of equality of opportunity. And finally, Americans have traditionally respected "doers"—men of action who got things done— more than thinkers, whose ideas were certainly unproductive, probably impractical, and possibly dangerous.

It is ironic that the weakening of the school's intellectual respon-

[6] Florence B. Stratemeyer, *et al.*, *Developing a Curriculum for Modern Living*, Bureau of Publications, Teachers College, Columbia University, 1957, pp. 155–65.
[7] Thomas H. Briggs, *Improving Instruction*, Macmillan, 1938, p. 219.

sibility can be attributed to two concepts that are themselves basically intellectual. Both science and democracy owe their progress to and depend for their advancement upon informed people with disciplined minds. Yet, inasmuch as both imply a rejection of certain forms of traditional authority, both also invite a questioning of traditional practices, in education as in other areas. Such questioning is desirable and, indeed, essential in a melioristic ideological climate in which "improvement" is not only hoped for and sought but confidently expected. This confidence is misplaced, however, if either scientific or democratic progress is expected in the absence of intellectual values. The basis of a free and technologically advanced society is the knowledge man has systematically accumulated and organized, together with the methods of inquiry and thought and the attitudes toward truth and freedom which constitute the intellectual tradition. Whatever else the modern secondary school may accomplish will be of little avail if intellectual development is neglected.

## INTELLECTUAL OBJECTIVES
## AND SUBSIDIARY CONCERNS

Joel H. Hildebrand, a distinguished chemist and a critic of American schools, has described the primary purpose of education as ". . . the fullest development within the capacity of every individual to think and act effectively through the mastery, by each student, to the extent of his ability, of the skills, knowledge, thought and appreciation which embody the major achievements of civilization." This brief statement recognizes that the cultural heritage is the source of the curriculum, that selection from this source is essential, that such selection requires judgment as to what achievements are "major," and that education is fundamentally concerned with individual development. It indicates further that the ultimate goals of education are effective thought and action, that individual attainments must be expected to differ, and that the outcomes of learning are knowledge, skills, and appreciations.

These assertions seem self-evident. Yet in the late 1950's observers both inside and outside education found it necessary to point out that the primary purpose of secondary schools is to promote intellectual development and that the familiar academic subjects offer the greatest potential for such development. Repeatedly it was emphasized that academically talented students should be encouraged and expected to develop their talents to the fullest, and that teachers should be scholars in their respective fields.

Actually, neither this viewpoint nor the need to state it was new. Thirty years earlier, in his 1926 Inglis lecture at Harvard University, Professor Paul Hanus had asserted that what was needed in the secondary schools of that day was ". . . *a militant attitude in favor of scholarship*—a serious intellectual purpose that is pervasive, insistent, and indomitable."[8] Hanus had declared, moreover, that ". . . to care for the superior pupil in a manner befitting his superiority is an imperative duty" and that "further to ensure recognition of and emphasis on scholarship among pupils requires corresponding emphasis on scholarship among teachers."[9]

Many attempts have been made to describe intellectual development. It is not easy to do. Presumably the aim of such development is what is often called an "educated man." Even among educated men, however, it would be difficult to get complete agreement on what an educated man is. When Sterling McMurrin was U.S. Commissioner of Education in the Kennedy Administration, he offered the following description:

> . . . An educated man is at home with ideas. He is as comfortable with concepts as he is with objects. He readily infers the general from the particular, for his capacities for rational abstraction equal his powers of concrete perception.
>
> An educated man is one whose reason disciplines his attitudes and action, but in whom the emotions are alive and sensitive and in whom there is genuine moral awareness, artistic perceptiveness, and spiritual commitment.
>
> An educated man has some understanding of himself. He is aware of his own prejudices, is critical of his own assumptions, and knows his own limitations.
>
> An educated man is aware of the events that have brought the world to where he finds it. He knows the wellsprings of his own society and culture and understands the essential unity of past, present, and future.
>
> An educated man has a fine sense of the relation of the ideal to the real, of the possible to the actual. He is not satisfied with the world as it is, but he knows that it will never be what he would like it to be. He has hope for the future but refuses to deny the tragedies of the present.
>
> An educated man has a cultivated curiosity that leads him beyond

[8] Paul Hanus, *Opportunity and Accomplishment in Secondary Education,* Harvard University Press, 1926, p. 46.

[9] *Ibid.,* p. 48.

the bounds of his own place and circumstance. Provincialism and parochialism have no place in his world, for they stifle thought and inhibit creativity.

Finally, an educated man is one who loves knowledge and will accept no substitutes and whose life is made meaningful through the never-ending process of the cultivation of his total intellectual resources.[10]

Whether even an "idea-centered" secondary school can develop a love of knowledge in "all of the children of all of the people" may be questioned. But the school cannot meet its intellectual responsibilities as an educational institution unless it places major emphasis on the development of significant concepts, rational processes, and transcendent values. Without these man is not truly free. And anything else a free society may expect of its secondary schools must be subordinate to the cultivation of free individuals. The only safeguard against the emergence of an "intellectual élite" is the existence of "intellectual masses." To stress intellectual cultivation with some students and other goals with the remainder is to perpetuate the dual system of earlier centuries.

In assigning priority to intellectual objectives one need not deny that other aspects of individual development are of concern to the school or that the school serves societal as well as individual aims. In the lecture quoted earlier, Hanus said,

> Of course, scholarship is not the sole aim of secondary education . . . for the inclusive aim of secondary education in this country, for all pupils at whatever stage their school learning may stop, is to lift the general level of our prospective citizens in health, knowledge, power, character, vocational efficiency and political judgment, whatever the native ability of individuals may be, above the level possible for elementary education; *to do this so as to make the most of every grade of ability including the highest.*[11]

The twentieth-century American high school has been called upon, and has permitted itself, to take on numerous objectives to meet both societal and individual needs. It may be argued that social institutions, being instituted by man, are legitimately subject to change at the hands of each generation to serve whatever purposes seem desirable. Largely through the mechanism of local lay control,

---

[10] Sterling McMurrin, "Some Basic Issues in Teacher Education," *Professional Imperatives: Expertness and Self-Determination*, Report of Conference of Commission on Teacher Education and Professional Standards, Fort Collins, Colorado, 1962, p. 14.

[11] Hanus, *op. cit.*, p. 51.

Americans have obviously been willing to change their schools in the hope of solving a variety of social problems. Moreover, the education profession, in its concern for the total welfare of children, has not only willingly acceded to public pressures on the school to broaden its aims but has often exerted pressure of its own on a reluctant or indifferent public in behalf of change.

There is no question but that the secondary school is expected to fulfill certain societal objectives. In making "The Great Investment"[12] in schooling, society properly expects commensurate returns. The question is whether society should expect immediate results or long-term gains, or, put differently, whether the school should substitute explicit training in the duties of citizenship and employment for general education aimed at the fullest possible cultivation of valued individual potentials. There may have been a day when early training was feasible, a day when most occupations were relatively simple and stable and when patriotic citizenship seemed, at least, to be relatively uncomplicated. If there was, that day is gone, and any realistic assessment of contemporary society can lead only to the conclusion that a high order of intellectual, esthetic, and moral understanding is essential to both enlightened, responsible citizenship and technological, vocational efficiency.

Aside from sharing in the general socialization of the young, the secondary school cannot reasonably be expected to serve as an instrument for social action or a solver of society's problems. These tasks belong to other social institutions and to educated citizens as individuals. The school cannot guarantee that its products will be immediately employable or vocationally successful, that they will vote intelligently or even vote at all, that they will maintain their health, sanity, and physical fitness, or that they will drive carefully, use their leisure constructively, be good parents, avoid divorce, respect minorities, or even love America. What the school should be able to assure society is that its graduates possess the basic understandings, skills, and values which increase the likelihood of their acting intelligently and responsibly in their various roles in life and of their profiting from further education or special training.

The secondary school is concerned with all aspects of individual development, including the physical, emotional, and social. Its total environment contributes to these lines of development. But the

[12] Thomas Briggs, *The Great Investment*, Harvard University Press, 1928.

school is not responsible for these aspects to the extent that it is responsible for the moral, esthetic, and intellectual. Similarly, the school is concerned with society's aims. Its very existence contributes to some of them. But the aims of the school are not the same as the aims of society. The school equips individuals to examine society's aims and to help in achieving them.

## OPERATIONAL FUNCTIONS

From time to time lists of the "functions" of the secondary school have been advanced. All too often these functions have been treated as goals in themselves. In some instances the term function has been used to designate the school's responsibility to provide certain program elements or operating conditions which are considered essential to the achievement of ultimate objectives. In others, the term has been used to refer to the by-products of schooling, the results that accrue when schools pursue their legitimate aims.

In 1918, Alexander Inglis of Harvard concluded that the secondary school serves adjustive, integrating, differentiating, propaedeutic, selective, and diagnostic functions. Thirty years later Gruhn and Douglass found that junior high schools emphasized six functions: integration, articulation, socialization, differentiation, exploration, and guidance. Some of the items in these two lists are the same, some have similar names but different meanings, and some have similar meanings but different names.

Under the *adjustive* or *adaptive* function Inglis included ". . . both the establishment of certain fixed habits of reaction, certain fixed standards and ideals, and also the development of a capacity to readjust adequately to the changing demands of life."[13] The similarity of this function to that stressed by the "life adjustment" movement of thirty years later is obvious.[14] Inglis recognized that some conditions of life would remain relatively stable while others would be radically altered. But he stressed the individual's ability to *accommodate* to existing and changing conditions rather than his power to initiate, shape, or resist changes in the social order. In defining the same function for the junior high school under the heading of "socialization," Gruhn and Douglass added the notion of

[13] Alexander Inglis, *Principles of Secondary Education*, Houghton Mifflin, 1918, p. 377.

[14] See Mauritz Johnson, Jr., "The Rise and Fall of Life Adjustment," *Saturday Review*, 44 (March 18, 1961), pp. 46–47.

". . . contributing to future developments and changes in that social order."[15]

When "adjustment" carries manipulatory, static, or passive connotations, it is unsatisfactory as a function of the school. One does not "adjust" people as if they were machines. Nor is an education focused on adaptation to the status quo very appropriate in an age of rapid change. And however inexorable change seems to be, however unimportant the individual seems to be in influencing it, the school ought at least to lead students to understand that creative, concerned, reasoning, discerning people have more chance of controlling the direction of change than those who merely "adjust" to it.

The term "integration" has been used in at least seven senses with respect to education. For Inglis the *integrating* function of the high school had a societal orientation and included ". . . the development of that amount of like-mindedness, of unity in thought, habits, ideals, and standards, requisite for social cohesion and social solidarity."[16] Gruhn and Douglass' integration function, on the other hand, refers to the integration of previously acquired learnings into wholesome behavior and also to the provision of further "broad, general and common education" which will lead to such behavior.[17]

By the differentiation function Gruhn and Douglass mean the same as Inglis did by his *differentiating* function—namely, taking advantage of the differences among individuals "for the purpose of determining social efficiency."[18] Individual differences are thus viewed as assets to be prized rather than as obstacles to be overcome. Together, the differentiation and integration functions exemplify both the dilemma and the dream of American society and its schools—unity with diversity. To what degree must education be common and behavior conforming for the sake of societal cohesiveness? To what extent can individuals be creative and different and their education tailored to their unique characteristics? The committee mentioned earlier declared that "with increasing specialization in any society comes a corresponding necessity for increased attention to unification."[19] Perhaps the greatest challenge the sec-

[15] William Gruhn and Harl Douglass, *The Modern Junior High School*, 2nd ed., Ronald, 1956, p. 32.

[16] Inglis, *op. cit.*, p. 377.

[17] Gruhn and Douglass, *op. cit.*, p. 31.

[18] Inglis, *op. cit.*, p. 378.

[19] Commission on the Reorganization of Secondary Education, *op. cit.*, p. 23.

ondary school faces is finding and maintaining a satisfactory balance between these two demands.

Two functions that Inglis included did not appear in Gruhn and Douglass' list, partly because they are less pertinent to the junior high school than to the upper secondary level and partly because they are not entirely in harmony with recent educational thought. These are the *propaedeutic* and the *selective* functions. The propaedeutic function has reference to preparation for further education. An educational philosophy that emphasizes the here and now tends to minimize preparation for a more or less distant future.

Leaders of the junior-high-school movement have sought to focus attention on the immediate needs, problems, and interests of young adolescents. They have resisted attempts by the senior high school to impose expectations or requirements upon the lower level and have considered the junior high school relatively exempt from the demands of college preparation with which the senior high school must reckon. Although junior high schools have accepted *articulation* as one of their most important functions, they have placed greater emphasis on the responsibility to effect a smooth transition from the level below than on the obligation to prepare students for higher levels.

Inglis commented that secondary schools in his day tended either to overestimate or underestimate the importance of the propaedeutic function. Certainly it is being overestimated when educational experiences are viewed solely as necessary hurdles rather than as valuable in their own right, as, for example, when students are led to believe that the only purpose for studying algebra is that it is a prerequisite for geometry and the only reason for studying geometry is that it is required for college admission. But certainly, too, it is ridiculous to deny that education is preparatory. Indeed, anticipation of future demands and preparation for them are marks of intelligent behavior.

The *selective* function refers to the secondary school's role in determining "who shall be educated"[20] and how. The negative aspect of selection is the elimination of students, either upon or before their completion of the high-school program. The positive aspect is related to the previously mentioned function of differentiation. Recognizing the individual's right to the education most appropriate

[20] See W. Lloyd Warner, Robert Havighurst, and Martin Loeb, *Who Shall Be Educated?*, Harper & Row, 1944.

for him, the school selectively determines which students have the potential for various kinds of education and hence for various social roles, and by differential treatment it encourages and assists each individual to realize his fullest potential.

The selective function is also closely related to Inglis' final one, which he called the *diagnostic* or *directive* function. In ascribing to the secondary school the obligation to give each student an ". . . opportunity to test out and explore his capacities and interests . . ." and to ". . . provide some direction and guidance therefor," Inglis epitomized two functions which have been prominent features of the junior-high-school movement: *guidance* and *exploration*. These functions have often been misinterpreted. They concern the school's obligation to help each student heed the ancient admonition, "Know thyself," and to plan his education and career accordingly. The guidance function entails more than the formulation of plans, however. It includes assisting students to cope with the problems they face in fulfilling their plans and particularly in taking maximum advantage of the opportunities the secondary school offers them. The meaning of this function is distorted when it is identified solely with the activities of a small group of guidance specialists, especially when these workers are viewed as omnipotent arbiters of students' lives. Similarly, the exploration function is misinterpreted when it is associated with desultory sampling of the school's offerings by students, rather than with the self-discovery that a coherent program of general education makes possible.

The ten functions discussed above should not be construed as the goals of secondary schools. Some of them represent conditions which must be present if the goals are to be achieved effectively. Others represent concomitant effects of achieving the goals. Thus, if secondary education is to be effective, the school must *articulate* with other levels; *differentiate* its program and procedures in accordance with variations among students; *diagnose* individual potentialities; permit students to *explore* their strengths, weaknesses, preferences, and aversions; and provide students with *guidance* regarding their personal problems and plans. But schools are not established to perform these functions; they perform such functions in order to realize their educational purposes more fully. Similarly, in the course of performing their primary educational function, they simultaneously perform other functions: they promote the *integration* of society and the *socialization* of its young; they equip the young to *adjust* to the demands of society and to *adapt* to changing demands; they *prepare* students for future experiences and to some extent *select* which students are to have various opportunities. But, again, these functions must not be confused with the school's main business of promoting the achievement of important learning outcomes.

## LEARNING OUTCOMES

Despite widespread disagreement on the proper goals and functions of the secondary school, it is obvious that the school achieves its purposes primarily through the learning process. Learning is often defined as a change in behavior resulting from experience. This definition invites misunderstanding. Learning may be viewed both as a process and as the result of that process. The process may occur in a group setting, but only individuals learn. In the process the individual has an experience, but the experience may be quite contrived and not a natural outgrowth of his ordinary "experience" in day-to-day living. In the learning experience the learner engages in some activity, but he is not necessarily overtly active. Indeed, overt activity unaccompanied by mental activity seldom results in learning. Furthermore, the activity must be directed at some kind of subject matter. A learning experience entails content as well as activity.

The results of the learning process are manifest in behavior. Schools customarily contrive testing situations designed to elicit behavior indicative of learning. The measure of learning is the extent to which behavior has changed. But merely because the behavior is not elicited does not mean that learning has not occurred. Furthermore, the individual's spontaneous behavior is not always altered whenever learning takes place. What does occur is a mental reorganization which makes modified behavior possible. A leading contemporary educational psychologist has defined learning as ". . . a change in human disposition or capability, which can be retained, and which is not simply ascribable to growth."[21] The immediate outcomes of learning are not behaviors but altered perceptions, conceptions, and dispositions to behave.

The school achieves its broad educational goals only as students acquire a multitude of specific learning outcomes. These outcomes are conventionally classified into three major types or domains: (1)

---

21 Robert M. Gagné, *The Conditions of Learning*, Holt, Rinehart & Winston, 1965, p. 5.

the *cognitive,* which includes intellectual skills and the understanding of facts, concepts, and generalizations; (2) the *psychomotor,* which consists of a variety of other skills, and (3) the *affective,* which encompasses attitudes, interests, appreciations, and values. These are merely the kinds of learning that can take place. Before school personnel can plan experiences intended to result in learning, they must identify the specific outcomes desired.

Within each domain the various kinds of outcome differ in complexity. Bloom and his associates[22] have analyzed the cognitive domain and have suggested that it consists of six major classes of objectives. Their first category is *knowledge,* and the remainder comprise various intellectual skills and abilities, namely, *comprehension, application, analysis, synthesis,* and *evaluation.*

The *affective* domain has been subjected to similar analysis by Krathwohl and others,[23] but the resulting categories represent stages more than types of learning. Thus, the acquisition of affective learning outcomes proceeds from mere attending through responding, valuing, and organizing, to the level at which the individual's behavior and personality are characterized by a particular value. The psychomotor domain has not yet been comparably studied. Nevertheless, it is easy to envision many types of skill which are taught in secondary schools. Skills, too, vary in complexity and in the degree of dexterity, coordination, and knowledge they require.

Although the existing taxonomies include numerous subclasses, even these categories represent *kinds* of outcome, not outcomes themselves. A staggering number of specific outcomes constitute the instructional goals of a six-year secondary-school program. French and his associates[24] identified 50 behavioral goals of general education in the secondary school, but even these were far too general to be of much help in planning and evaluating instruction. It is easy for a secondary-school teacher to become so absorbed in the teaching of his subject that he loses sight of the broader goals of the institution. Nevertheless, in any consideration of the objectives and functions of secondary education, the "forests" of general aims must

[22] Benjamin Bloom, ed., *Taxonomy of Educational Objectives: The Cognitive Domain,* Longmans, Green, 1955.

[23] David Krathwohl, *et al., Taxonomy of Educational Objectives: The Affective Domain,* David McKay, 1964.

[24] Will French, *et al., Behavioral Goals for General Education in High School,* Russell Sage Foundation, 1957.

eventually be translated into the "trees" of specific learning outcomes.

Professional test-makers have long been aware that objectives must be very specific, not only to make it possible to construct test items but to provide a basis for sampling adequately the content of a course or subject. The need for such specificity is especially acute in the new art of "programed" instruction. Mager has defined an instructional objective as ". . . a statement of what the learner is to be like when he has successfully completed a learning experience."[25] This statement must define the conditions under which the acquired "terminal behavior" of the learner is expected to occur, and it must specify the criteria of acceptable performance.[26] Not every educator would agree that all learning can be programed or, indeed, evaluated. Some would object to stating all instructional goals behavioristically. But most would probably agree that there is a vast difference between describing the objectives of secondary education in such broad terms as self-cultivation, vocational competence, and responsible citizenship on the one hand and, on the other, in such specific terms as knowing the five regular polyhedrons, being able to focus a microscope, and acquiring a defensible attitude toward capital punishment.

Theoretically, specific objectives can be deduced from more general ones. Actually, such deduction seldom occurs. More often specific objectives are proposed and then defended by showing their relevance to broader goals. Purposes can be pursued from one level of immediacy to a higher level by repetitively asking the question, "Why?" Eventually, the ultimate purpose one is willing to accept is reached. Failure to recognize differences in the level of discourse leads to almost as much confusion as do actual differences of opinion regarding the purposes of secondary education. Another source of confusion is lack of clarity regarding *whose* purposes are under discussion: those of the students who receive the education, those of the professional people who provide it, those of the specific community that supports it, or those of the wider society that encourages it.

More significant in the long run, however, than the particular purposes for which secondary schooling is offered and acquired may be the ways in which it can be used. Whether it is in work or in play,

---

25 Robert Mager, *Preparing Objectives for Programmed Instruction,* Fearon Publishers, 1961, p. 3.
    26 *Ibid.,* p. 12.

in the discharge of civic duties or family responsibilities, that a given learning eventually proves useful may be as inconsequential as it is unpredictable. What is important for educational planning is the realization that learnings are likely to be used in one of four different ways. Whatever purpose they serve, certain skills and facts will be used *replicatively*—that is, in the same manner as they were learned. On the other hand, many facts will be used only *associatively*. Though imperfectly recalled, they are evoked as a flood of somehow related, vaguely relevant notions, and they serve to enrich an experience in a way that would be impossible had the facts not earlier been encountered. Except by specialists, Broudy, Smith, and Burnett point out,[27] few concepts and generalizations learned in school will be used *applicatively* in the solution of problems; nonspecialists are more likely to use them *interpretatively* in understanding problems and situations.

The chief objective of general education, therefore, is to equip individuals to interpret subsequent experiences correctly. If secondary education is viewed primarily as general education, the outcomes of which are used chiefly interpretatively, then the secondary school must give students opportunities to engage in logical operations on organized content consisting of descriptive and evaluative concepts and ideas, carefully selected for their explanatory power. The acquisition of powerful understandings and the ability to use them interpretatively are the essence of intellectual development. As Bloom and his colleagues put it,

> . . . We have the task of preparing individuals for problems that cannot be foreseen in advance, and about all that can be done under such conditions is to help the student acquire generalized intellectual abilities and skills which will serve him well in many new situations. This places faith in the intellectual virtues as providing some form of stability for the individual who must find or make some order in his world.[28]

## Suggestions for Class Discussion and Further Investigation

1. Find out about the "Old Deluder Satan" Act, which was passed in the Massachusetts Bay Colony in 1647. Did it provide for free compulsory secondary education? What did it seek to compel?

[27] Harry Broudy, B. O. Smith, and Joe Burnett, *Democracy and Excellence in American Secondary Education,* Rand McNally, 1964.
[28] Bloom, *op. cit.,* p. 40.

2. Try to get from written sources some of the flavor of what a Latin grammar school must have been like. What did these schools teach? How did they teach it? Who was Ezekiel Cheever? What was the greatest number of Latin grammar schools ever to exist in colonial America? What was the state of secondary education at the time of the Revolution?

3. What did Benjamin Franklin have in mind for his academy? How do you think he would have reacted had he been around in 1821 when the Boston English Classical School was established to provide ". . . an education that shall fit [the student] for active life, and shall serve as a foundation for eminence in his profession, whether mercantile or mechanical . . ."?

4. Why have "rate bills" so often been referred to as "infamous"? What effect did their abolishment have on secondary education? How was this effect related to that of the "Kalamazoo Case"?

5. What kind of people served on the Committee of Ten? What subjects did they have in mind when they agreed that ". . . for purposes of general education, one study is as good as another . . ." and therefore ". . . the choice of subjects in secondary schools is a matter of comparative indifference"? Is this statement consistent with the "faculty psychology–mental discipline" viewpoint?

6. Does the secondary school face a genuine dilemma in attempting to provide education that is both common for all and different for each? Consider how each of the following dualisms relates to this basic issue:

> unification—specialization
> unity—diversity
> heritage—change
> integration—differentiation
> loyalty—liberty
> conviction—toleration
> cooperation—competition

7. In a class or other group try to get agreement on five to ten specific things that all secondary students should learn. Classify each item by domain (cognitive, psychomotor, or affective) and by probable use (replicative, associative, applicative, or

interpretative). Is it possible to predict in which aspect of life (for example, maintaining health, using leisure time, family living, citizenship, vocation) each will be of value? Try to think of a learning outcome representative of each domain, manner of use, and life activity that was not represented in the original list.

## Suggestions for Further Reading

A quick overview of secondary education from ancient Greece to modern America may be found in Chapter 14 of John S. Brubacher's *History of the Problems of Education* (McGraw-Hill, 1947). William M. French provides brief accounts of the Latin grammar school and the academy in Chapters 3 and 4 of *American Secondary Education* (Odyssey, 1957). More detailed descriptions of these institutions and the early high schools are given in Elmer Ellsworth Brown's *The Making of Our Middle Schools* (Longmans, Green, 1921) and Emit D. Grizzel's *Origin and Development of the High School in New England Before 1865* (Macmillan, 1923).

Examine the complete original versions of several pronouncements on secondary education in order to get their full intent and significance. The basic ones include the National Education Association's *Report of the Committee of Ten on Secondary School Studies* (American Book Co., 1894); the pamphlet on the *Cardinal Principles of Secondary Education* (U.S. Bureau of Education, Bulletin 1918, No. 35, Reprinted 1937); the report by Thomas H. Briggs and others on "Functions of Secondary Education," *Bulletin of the Department of Secondary-School Principals,* Vol. 21, No. 64 (January, 1937); and three Educational Policies Commission reports, published by the National Education Association. These are *The Purposes of Education in American Democracy* (1938), *Education for All American Youth* (1944), and *The Central Purpose of American Education* (1961). Herbert Spencer's essay, "What Knowledge Is of Most Worth?" which seems to have been a basis for several of these statements, is included in a collection by Ronald Gross entitled *The Teacher and the Taught* (Dell, 1963).

All teachers should be familiar with the *Taxonomy of Educational Objectives*. Handbook I, *Cognitive Domain* (Longmans, Green, 1956), was edited for a committee by Benjamin S. Bloom;

Handbook II, *Affective Domain* (David McKay, 1964), was prepared by David R. Krathwohl and others. Also relevant are the analysis by Will French and associates, *Behavioral Goals of General Education in High School* (Russell Sage Foundation, 1957), and Robert F. Mager's little book, *Preparing Objectives for Programmed Instruction* (Fearon Publishers, 1961).

There are many lengthy and comprehensive textbooks on secondary education. Two that have been especially influential were cited in the text of this chapter: Alexander Inglis' *Principles of Secondary Education* (Houghton Mifflin, 1918) and *The Modern Junior High School*, 2nd ed., by William T. Gruhn and Harl R. Douglass (Ronald, 1956). A more recent comprehensive treatment is given by Lindley J. Stiles, Lloyd E. McCleary, and Roy C. Turnbaugh in *Secondary Education in the United States* (Harcourt, Brace & World, 1964). But the most provocative proposals for changing the secondary schools are to be found in *Democracy and Excellence in American Secondary Education,* by Harry S. Broudy, B. Othanel Smith, and Joe R. Burnett (Rand McNally, 1964).

## Chapter Two

# Organization

There is an inherent antagonism between scholarship and institutional organization. Scholarship demands freedom and encourages creativity; organization imposes authority and requires conformity. If a secondary school is to achieve its objectives, no matter what they are, its administrators must understand what conditions promote learning and scholarship, and its teachers must understand what organizational arrangements are essential to the attainment of institutional goals.

Not only are there various types of secondary school; within each type, organization varies considerably. It is not, therefore, a simple matter to describe either the internal organization of secondary schools or the larger structure of which they are a part.

### TYPES OF SECONDARY SCHOOL

Approximately six out of seven American secondary schools are public institutions. Nevertheless, over a million students attend secondary schools that are not publicly supported or controlled. These nonpublic schools are often classified as "private," although this term is sometimes reserved for *independent* schools which are not under the direct control of a religious denomination. Such schools are the modern-day academies. Some of them resemble the public schools in being day schools[1] that serve a definite geographic area. Many, however, are boarding schools that accept pupils from a large region or from the entire nation. About 30 per cent of all nonpublic secondary schools have boarding facilities. Since boarding schools have 24-hour control over their students, they are able to supervise study and emphasize character formation in the manner of their counterparts, the "public" secondary schools of England.

[1] The Crane School in Harney County, Oregon, is reported by *Life* Magazine (October 16, 1950, p. 117) to be the only public boarding school in the United States except for certain Indian Schools.

Most independent schools stress college-preparatory work and hence are known as "prep" schools. Many are selective in their admissions and maintain high academic standards. Undoubtedly, some serve as convenient repositories for unruly or unwanted children of well-to-do families. In egalitarian America private schools have been popularly viewed as snobbish status symbols, but many offer scholarship and jobs to well-qualified students from families of lower socioeconomic standing. Like their public counterparts, private schools differ so greatly among themselves that generalizations about them are misleading and often unfair.

Some independent schools are exceedingly poor in the quality of their facilities, faculty, and results. Others are well endowed in all respects. Some are relatively new, while others, like the Phillips Academies at Andover and Exeter, were founded in the days of the American Revolution, forty years before the first public high school was established in Boston. Although private schools are often thought of as traditional in program and methods, some of them have pioneered "progressive" educational practices, and many are still in the forefront of experimentation and innovation.[2] Indeed, the very fact that they are independent gives them a freedom to define objectives and to devise programs and procedures which is not enjoyed by schools that are publicly supported and controlled.

The administrators of independent schools are customarily known as headmasters instead of principals; the teachers are often called masters; and the guidance counselors may have the title of dean. Usually each residence at a boarding school is presided over by a teacher serving as housemaster. The policies of an independent school are generally established by a board of trustees.

A dozen or more religious denominations sponsor schools. Four out of five nonpublic secondary schools are church-related, and 60 per cent of these have Roman Catholic affiliation. Roman Catholic secondary schools may be parochial, serving a single parish, or diocesan, serving a number of parishes. Most dioceses have a diocesan superintendent of schools who is in charge of all education below the collegiate level. Catholic secondary schools are usually four-year institutions preceded by an eight-year elementary program, although three-year junior high schools are not unknown.

---

2 See, for example, David Mallery, *New Approaches in Education: A Study of Experimental Programs in Independent Schools,* National Council of Independent Schools, Boston, 1961.

Many different combinations of grades qualify an institution as a secondary school. Most common are the junior-senior high school (grades 7–12), the regular high school (9–12), the senior high school (10–12), and the junior high school (7–9 or 7–8). The nineteenth-century high school was a four-year institution with entrance limited to elementary-school graduates. Most elementary schools consisted of eight grades, though in some southern states, from Reconstruction days until recently, a seven-grade elementary program prevailed, and in some New England states nine grades were included for a time.

The elementary and secondary schools had quite independent origins, and in the days of the Latin grammar school and the early academy they were parallel, rather than consecutive, institutions. To enter a Latin school or an academy a child did not have to attend elementary school at all, and, indeed, those children who continued in the elementary school were those who did not intend to go to secondary school. The distinction between the two institutions was less a matter of the pupil's age than of the affluence and station of his parents.

As elementary schools grew in number and size during the early nineteenth century, they were organized into grades. The number of grades eventually settled on was eight, as in the greatly admired Prussian schools of that era. Graduation from eighth grade became a worthy goal for the majority of children and a requirement for entry to the academy or high school. In New York State the first of the well-known Regents examinations were designed to confirm the eligibility of elementary-school graduates for admission to secondary schools. These "preliminary" Regents examinations were administered at the end of the eighth grade well into the 1950's, even though for many years previously a reorganized secondary school beginning with grade seven had had official endorsement.

The impetus for the reorganization movement is usually credited to Charles Eliot, the former president of Harvard University who is also known for his promotion of the elective system at the college level. For twenty years, beginning in 1872, he agitated for some kind of reform in the lower schools which would effect an "economy of time" in preparing students for college. In 1892, as chairman of the National Education Association's Committee of Ten, he finally had an opportunity to explore the possibilities of beginning secondary instruction earlier. Subcommittees representing nine academic subjects were appointed. Each subcommittee, except the one for Greek, recommended that its subject be introduced one to two years before the first year of high school. Alternatively, the Committee of Ten suggested that the last two elementary grades be made a part of the secondary school. This suggestion was debated by numerous other committees and commissions during the following twenty years. While the debates continued, various districts shuffled the grades around, attaching the eighth to the high school here, placing the seventh and eighth in a separate building there, and finally, in 1909, forming a three-year intermediate school consisting of grades seven, eight, and nine. This was the first junior high school. Whether that school was in Columbus, Ohio, or Berkeley, California, is a matter of interpretation.

For half a century the reorganization of secondary education from a four- to a six-year format proceeded. By 1960 over three-quarters of the secondary schools, enrolling more than 80 per cent of the nation's students, were of the reorganized variety. The last of the above-mentioned series of national committees, a Commission on the Reorganization of Secondary Education, had been appointed in 1913. Its "cardinal principles" report, issued in 1918, provided a blueprint for a new institution encompassing more grades and broader functions than had characterized the high school described by the Committee of Ten a quarter of a century earlier. In the postwar period of the 1920's, growing high-school enrollments and attendant building problems created favorable conditions for applying the blueprint. Junior and senior high schools sprang up in many of the larger cities and towns. Newly consolidated or centralized rural districts, in which separate units were not feasible, were required, or at least encouraged, to form undivided six-year secondary units.

The depression of the 1930's and the war of the following decade slowed the reorganization process, but the pace picked up again in the second postwar period. Newly created or rapidly growing suburbs found it convenient to concentrate first on elementary schools, and then as the children grew older, to establish junior high schools, delaying the senior high school as long as possible. Similarly, when growing enrollments forced communities with six-year schools to build additional facilities, they often elected to separate the junior and senior levels rather than form duplicate six-year units.

In the undivided six-year secondary school, the four-year high school is often preserved as the dominant feature, with the two lower grades treated as adjuncts. The principal change for these grades as they passed from elementary to secondary status seems often to have been merely the replacement of the self-contained classroom by a system of departmentalization, in which each subject is taught by a different teacher. In the smaller schools, however, the teachers of grades seven and eight frequently do not participate in the departmental activities of the high school, nor are they able to carry on such activities by themselves. Moreover, their pupils often are left out of student activities, or, if they are allowed to participate in the high-school program, they are usually overshadowed by the older students. An undivided six-year school encompasses young children of twelve and mature youths of eighteen—an age span that many educators regard as too wide. At the same time, many feel that two grades are too few, inasmuch as pupils enter one year and leave the next. Three- or four-year units with distinct programs, if not separate facilities, seem to be most feasible during these years when students are moving from childhood through adolescence to virtual adulthood.

The most widely advocated organization for secondary education consists of a three-year junior high school and a three-year senior high school. In the classic arrangement, which is possible only in the larger centers, the senior high school draws its students from two or three junior high schools, each of which is fed by five or six elementary schools. Each of the feeder schools contains two sixth-grade sections of 25 to 30 pupils; each junior high school receives, therefore, 250 to 350 new seventh-graders each year, making its enrollment, after some allowance for dropping out, somewhere between 650 and 900. The senior high school admits 350 to 600 tenth-graders and has a total enrollment of 900 to 1500 students. This arrangement permits the smaller children to attend the schools nearest their homes. Moreover, enrollments at the secondary levels are large enough to enable the schools to offer a broad program conducted by specialized personnel using specialized facilities.

In an educational system that is divided into three distinct units there is some danger that pupils will be subjected to abrupt changes as they move from one level to the next. One of the arguments for the junior high school is that it serves as an articulating unit between the elementary school and the high school proper. It introduces students gradually to the procedures and expectations of the secondary school. Thus, the middle unit "bridges the gap" between the two institutions, which, despite their separate historical origins and their different sources of teachers, had been joined together in the 8–4 system.

Some critics object that setting up a junior high school exacerbates the problem by creating two breaks where there was only one before. They argue for an uninterrupted twelve-year school, on the grounds that growth and learning are continuous processes. The defenders of the three-level plan do not deny that this continuity exists, but they hold that just as children and adolescents differ sufficiently to warrant different educational treatment, students need to be treated still differently during the transition from childhood to adolescence. Furthermore, in this period of uncertain developmental status, students achieve a sense of identity from sharing in a school unit of their own.

The argument for a separate middle-school unit is weakened somewhat, however, by the fact that the time at which this transition occurs differs greatly from individual to individual and between the sexes. Any middle school will inevitably contain a mixture consisting of immature children, primarily boys; relatively mature young people, primarily girls; and those of both sexes who are in the "in-between" stage. But this weakness is not unique to the junior high school. No institutional arrangement designed for groups can be completely appropriate for every individual. By serving the group with maximum diversity, the middle unit permits the elementary school to cater primarily to children and the senior high school mainly to adolescents.

There will probably always be variations in the organizational pattern of secondary schools in the United States. It seems unlikely that the distinction between elementary and secondary education will disappear entirely or that any grades will be returned to the elementary school. Rather, the secondary school will probably begin at an even lower grade, thus making a middle school even more essential if a manageable age range is to be maintained. But whether this middle school includes grades 6–8 or 5–8 or continues to serve grades 7–9, it must have well-defined purposes and its own identity and at the same time assure continuity with the adjacent units.

The junior-high-school program is one of general education. Although all pupils do not pursue identical programs, neither do they have a large number of options available to them. Senior high schools are more likely to provide a variety of programs for students with different characteristics and purposes. Some large systems have established separate schools for each kind of program—academic, vocational, performing arts, technical, and the like. Most systems, however, either by choice or necessity, maintain *comprehensive* or cosmopolitan high schools which offer diversified programs and serve the entire spectrum of students. This is a difficult assignment. James B. Conant, former president of Harvard University, found only eight such schools out of more than a hundred surveyed that, by his standards, were doing an adequate job for all kinds of students.[3] Nevertheless, he concluded that the comprehensive high school needed to be improved, not abolished.

Since it is difficult for schools with fewer than a hundred students in the graduating class to offer sufficiently comprehensive programs, district reorganization is urgently needed to create larger schools. In 1958, about 80 per cent of American high schools had fewer than 90 students in the graduating class and 29 per cent enrolled fewer than a hundred in all grades. Even if it were decided that all young people could best be served by a common nonvocational program of secondary education, many of the smaller high schools would still be unable to provide a broad enough program to accommodate all variations in student ability. The need for district reorganization would be greatly decreased, however, if less diversified programs were offered.

In areas where the population is sparse, it is often impracticable to create larger schools. Small schools can broaden their programs, however, by using such devices as educational television, programed instruction, correspondence courses, multiple-subject classes, alternate-year offerings, and the sharing of teachers with the nearest school. Some states have created shared-services boards through which a number of participating systems can jointly employ teaching personnel and other specialists for part-time service in their schools.

## ADMINISTRATIVE UNITS

Most public secondary schools operate within a school district organization. In some states the school districts are coterminous with some political unit, such as a county, town, or city; in others they are not. Some districts do not operate a secondary school of their own. Instead, they contract to have their pupils educated in a

[3] James B. Conant, *The American High School Today*, McGraw-Hill, 1959, p. 22.

neighboring district, which may have one secondary school or, as in New York City, several hundred.

School districts are usually governed by some kind of board of education or school committee. The members of the board may be elected directly in a district election, or elected on the regular political ballot, or appointed by a governmental official, usually a mayor. Most districts are fiscally independent—that is, they establish their own budgets and levy taxes. Large city districts, may, however, be dependent on the municipal government for approval of their budgets and for their share of public funds. Even in the smaller towns of some states, such as Connecticut, the board of education cannot levy taxes to meet its budget; this power resides in another group, the board of finance.

Usually the administrative head of a district's school system is called a superintendent of schools, although the titles "supervising principal" and "district principal" are not uncommon. In any case, this chief school administrator is directly responsible for the execution of the school board's policies. In a large district the superintendent is assisted by a central office staff of professional and clerical workers, including assistant superintendents, business managers, various coordinators and directors, subject-specialist supervisors, and special service personnel, such as psychologists, physicians, and nurses. In a small district the chief school officer may have no assistance whatever. Indeed, he may also serve as the principal of the only school in the district.

These two functions are distinct, however. The chief school administrator directs the over-all organization of which the school is a part; the principal directs the internal organization of a particular school.

Again according to the size of the school, the staff available to a principal may range from none at all to a sizable group of assistant principals or vice principals, guidance specialists, and health personnel. In a large school, the heads of departments are also administrators, serving in a "line" (authoritative) relation rather than in a "staff" (advisory) relation with respect to the teachers.

Because of the historical origin of his position as "principal teacher" and because of his own professional beginnings as a teacher, the principal of a school usually identifies closely with his faculty. At the same time he must, as an administrator, represent the interests and wishes of the lay authorities to whom he is responsible. Obviously, these two loyalties are often in conflict. Teachers should recognize the difficulties inherent in the administrative role.

In any organization an administrator performs external and internal functions. The external function is representative. The principal must represent his school in dealing with those who control its sources of support. On the one hand, he is expected by his staff members to defend the school's standards, integrity, and results, and, on the other, to wrest from higher echelons in the organization the facilities and conditions they need to do their job.

Internally, the principal must allocate resources equitably, establish and enforce rules and procedures to keep the school operating efficiently, and demand of his staff whatever performance is necessary to ensure that institutional goals are met. He must hire only those people who seem likely to perform satisfactorily, try to retain those who do, and discharge those who prove inadequate. Finally, he must motivate teachers and other staff personnel to innovate and go beyond the minimal demands of their assignments to higher levels of performance.

Ordinary "fringe benefits" which may serve to attract and retain staff members are inadequate in motivating individual initiative and creativity. Some administrators are apparently "goal-oriented," stressing production and effective performance directly. Others appear to focus on promoting group cohesiveness and gratifying individual needs, on the assumption that satisfied teachers will be productive teachers. Used exclusively, neither approach is likely to be effective. Teachers must of course be treated as people, not production units, but where everyone is satisfied, comfortable, and friendly there may be little incentive to change procedures and improve performance. The key seems to be for the teacher to identify himself with organizational goals, so that achieving them is personally rewarding. This is why teachers should understand the secondary school as an institution, participate in determining its goals and procedures, have the freedom and support they need to try new ideas, and receive some recognition for their efforts to do a superior job. The perceptive teacher will recognize that the organizational problems he faces in his relations with students are similar to those the administrator faces in relation to teachers and that similar considerations apply in motivating achievement.

INTERNAL ORGANIZATION

In small secondary schools the internal organization is very simple. Here each teacher is directly responsible to the principal. Teachers carry out their teaching assignments independently, with only incidental regard for the activities of their colleagues. Larger schools are organized by departments, and the individual teacher deals with the administration only through his department chairman or head. The chairman supervises the teachers in his department and shares with them responsibility for the adequacy of the curriculum and the quality of the instruction. In some secondary schools, particularly junior high schools, all the teachers of each grade may also meet under a chairman to consider the entire program for that grade.

Some very large schools have adopted another form of organization which goes under various names: the little school, the school-within-a-school, the house plan, and others. Under this system the student body is divided into two or more subschools or houses, each with its own administrator, faculty, and program. Usually each "little school" includes two or three grades, though in some cases each grade is treated as a school in itself. Dividing a large school into subunits preserves the more intimate atmosphere and personal attention of a small school; at the same time, it affords the more extensive facilities and greater efficiency of a large one. The staff of the subschool is encouraged to act as a team. Confusingly enough, the term "team teaching," which is also used to designate a quite different organization, is often applied to this kind of arrangement.

Team teaching is more commonly associated with a scheme suggested by staff utilization studies carried out in the late 1950's for the National Association of Secondary-School Principals. Often called the "Trump plan," after the man who led the studies; this scheme is designed to use teachers' talents more effectively and to make students more responsible for their own learning, chiefly through more flexible scheduling and grouping. In each subject field, teaching teams consisting of a team leader, teachers, interns, and subprofessional personnel assume joint responsibility for teaching a large number of students through the judicious use of total-group instruction, small-group discussions, and independent study. The team is expected, through careful planning, to make the most effective use of the specialized knowledge and teaching skills of each member.[4]

4 See J. Lloyd Trump and Dorsey Baynham, *Focus on Change: A Guide to Better Schools*, Rand McNally, 1961.

The contrast is evident between this arrangement and the conventional one in which the teacher plans independently and teaches all topics in a course to relatively small sections. Also evident is its similarity to the college program in which a senior professor lectures twice a week, assistants or junior instructors meet small recitation groups on another day, and the students work independently on outside assignments the rest of the week.

## GROUPING OF STUDENTS

It is conventional in American secondary schools to assign students to grades and then to instructional sections and homeroom groups. When all students follow identical programs, as is sometimes the case in grades seven and eight, instructional sections and homeroom groups often coincide. In cases where students follow different programs, homeroom groups may be formed with a view to achieving a cross section of the students in a given grade. Students may be assigned to a homeroom randomly, alphabetically, or by an even more deliberate effort to achieve heterogeneity. Seldom do homeroom groups cut across grade lines, though some junior-high-school principals maintain that when a third of the group is drawn from each grade, the older students help orient the new ones and tend to behave more responsibly.

Educators disagree over what is the most desirable composition of instructional sections, and changes in fashion occur periodically. Early in the present century the high school served a fairly homogeneous group, and the need for sectioning according to ability was not so great as it was later to become. During the 1920's and 1930's the diversity of the student body increased, standardized tests became available, and grouping by ability or achievement was widely practiced. In the next two decades such grouping was frowned upon as undemocratic and inimical to mental health. By 1960 it was again considered essential to individual opportunity and the national interest.

Grouping by ability can do nothing in itself for the individual student's achievement. What it can do is to make it possible to provide different content, use different methods, proceed at a different pace, and set different standards for different groups in the same grade. But if the groups are made different and then treated identically, few if any benefits can be expected. In a vast number of schools no appropriate adaptation of content and methods is made; so it is not surprising that research reveals little relation between the homogeneity of groups and students' achievement.[5] Since there is some risk that ability grouping may engender undesirable social attitudes and self-concepts, it is perhaps unwise for schools to follow the practice if they have no intention of making the necessary adaptations.

Grouping plans vary greatly. There is a vast difference between a plan that creates three or four levels within a grade, with a suitable version of courses for each level, and a plan that attempts to divide a grade into 10 to 20 narrow ability bands. It is impossible even to detect such small differences, much less to adapt programs to them. Before a group with special characteristics is formed, there should be some specific course or program for it. The proper basis for forming groups for some subjects may be quite different from that for other subjects. For some subjects heterogeneous groups may be most appropriate. That grouping should, so far as scheduling permits, be done subject by subject rather than for a student's entire program is widely advocated but less widely observed in practice. In small schools it is almost impossible.

Whenever elective courses are available, as in the senior high school, an automatic grouping process tends to operate. Because of the realities of scheduling practices, even when ability grouping is not intended, students who choose the same electives often find themselves in the same sections in the required subjects as well. When the range of ability or achievement within class sections is deliberately reduced, the basis used should be identifiable and should be relevant to the instruction to be offered. The relatively high positive correlation among abilities means that groups which are made homogeneous with respect to one kind of ability tend to be somewhat homogeneous with respect to another. On the other hand, the common practice of averaging a variety of somewhat disparate factors, such as school marks, measures of scholastic ability, reading levels, and arithmetic scores, usually results in a grouping that is homogeneous with respect to nothing that can be identified. Employing multiple attributes as bases is not the same, however, as using multiple evidences of a single attribute selected as the basis for grouping. Combining test scores, previous marks, and teachers' judg-

---

[5] Jason Millman and Mauritz Johnson, Jr., "Relation of Section Variance to Achievement Gains in English and Mathematics in Grades 7 and 8," *American Educational Research Journal*, I (January, 1964), pp. 47–51.

ments relating to the same factor may increase the reliability of the estimate.

There can be no perfect system of grouping students. As we said earlier, *no institutional arrangement designed for groups can be completely appropriate for every individual.* Just as curriculum adaptation should precede grouping, instructional adaptation should follow it. Indeed, if teachers assume that the existence of some plan for reducing the heterogeneity of class sections relieves them of the need to differentiate instruction in the classroom, it would be far better to have no such plan at all. But given proper understanding by teachers, any administrative procedure that can make the instructional task more manageable for them is certainly to be desired, unless it has undesired side effects.

Under the Trump plan, the large number of students assigned to a teaching team can readily be grouped and regrouped to serve various purposes. What is more, the decisions on group composition can be made by those who have the responsibility for instruction—the teachers themselves.

This kind of flexibility in grouping does not necessitate team teaching, however. Some secondary principals have adopted the practice of assigning two or three teachers to teach that many sections of the same course during the same period, leaving it to the teachers themselves to determine which pupils should comprise each section and to transfer pupils from one section to another when appropriate. This practice cannot be followed in schools that have too few teachers in each subject. In extremely small schools that have only one section per grade, grouping of any kind is impossible unless the notion of grades is abandoned.

The idea of grades in secondary schools is an inheritance from the elementary school. What is now known as the tenth grade was, prior to reorganization, the second or sophomore *year* of high school, and of course it is still frequently referred to in that way. Actually, the concept of grade is not so important in the ninth and subsequent grades, in which promotion is usually subject by subject, as it is in grades seven and eight, in which the elementary-school practice of promotion by grade is common. In the elective subjects of the senior high school it is not uncommon for students in different grades to be in the same class. Required courses are usually restricted to a single grade, however, no matter how many group levels there are in a course.

By ignoring grade designations in, say, grades seven and eight, a small school which normally has only one or two sections per grade can form from two to four instructional groups, thereby reducing the range of ability or achievement in each group. Such ungraded groups encompass a somewhat greater chronological age range than do groups limited to a single grade, but this causes no serious difficulties. More bothersome is the necessity of modifying the curriculum sequence to conform to a two-year cycle. Nevertheless, ungrading the secondary school may make it possible to form more appropriate instructional groups than does the observance of grade distinctions.

Grade designations may be retained for administrative and social purposes, but for instruction a nongraded organization in which each subject field is divided into ten or twelve or even more levels not identified with any of the six secondary years might ensure each student a well-defined course suited to his needs. Students who would conventionally be in several adjacent grades might then be assigned to the same level for instruction. Brown[6] has described in detail how his high school successfully eliminated grades by organizing subjects into five numerically designated "phases" that increase in depth from remedial work to college-level advanced-placement courses. The program includes two additional alphabetically designated phases: a "Quest phase" for students with exceptional talents in a specific area, and "Phase X" for nonacademic subjects in which students need not move to another phase in order to work at an individually appropriate level.

Despite such occasional innovations, traditional organizational patterns persist in most secondary schools. Generations of students pass through the schools, and teachers come and go, but the organization endures. Teachers are typically not greatly interested in organizational questions. They do not like to think of themselves as "organization men." In their view organization is a problem for administrators, and many other educational problems seem far more significant.

Nevertheless, mass education must be organized, and the organization ought to promote both efficiency and quality. A reexamination of familiar patterns is called for. Where schools are too small, district reorganization needs to be considered. Schools that are excessively large may need to be subdivided. Where departments do not exist, they need to be formed. Teachers may have to give up some of

6 B. Frank Brown, *The Nongraded High School*, Prentice-Hall, 1963.

their independence and isolation and join their colleagues on teaching teams. Irrational and inflexible grouping plans need to be revised. Grades may need to be eliminated. By resisting proposals for organizational change, teachers may unknowingly prevent the establishment of the only conditions under which secondary education of the quality they themselves want to offer can be provided.

*Suggestions for Class Discussion and Further Investigation*

1. Nonpublic schools have been called a divisive force in our society. Do you agree? Should they be abolished, or encouraged? If their enrollments, now between 10 and 15 per cent of total enrollments, should begin to increase rapidly, at what point would you become concerned?

2. Muster arguments for and against each of the following organizational arrangements:

    Regular high school (8–4) vs. reorganized secondary school (6–6).

    Undivided junior–senior high school (6–6) vs. separate junior and senior high schools (6–3–3).

    Three-year junior high school (6–3–3) vs. two-year junior high school (6–2–4).

    Three-year junior high school (6–3–3) vs. "middle school" (5–3–4) or (4–4–4).

3. Which is more reasonable—to judge the comprehensiveness of a secondary school by the diversity of its program or by the extent to which it admits all those in its attendance area who are in the appropriate age group?

4. School personnel are "authorities" in two different senses. How do these two sources of authority relate to the distinction between line and staff relationships?

5. What are the advantages and disadvantages of smallness in a secondary school? Of largeness? How large would a junior high school have to be in order for the "house" plan to be feasible?

*Suggestions for Further Reading*

The United States Office of Education, currently a part of the Department of Health, Education and Welfare, is responsible for maintaining statistics relating to American education. Two USOE bulletins summarize the status of secondary schools: Edmund A. Ford and Virgil R. Walker, *Public Secondary Schools,*

Statistics of Education in the United States, No. 1 (Government Printing Office, 1961), and Diane B. Gertler, *Statistics of Non-public Secondary Schools, 1960–61* (Government Printing Office, 1963). Since these bulletins will in time be superseded, the latest versions should be consulted for a factual and graphic description of the current organization of secondary education.

The reorganization movement in secondary education is discussed in several books about the junior high school. Leonard V. Koos, whose career spanned several decades of the movement, described it in retrospect in the first chapter of his *Junior High School Trends* (Harper, 1955). A more recent and comprehensive textbook is *Modern Education for the Junior High School Years* (Bobbs-Merrill, 1961) by William Van Til, Gordon F. Vars, and John Lounsbury.

The comprehensive high school was the subject of the first of James B. Conant's several reports on education, *The American High School Today* (McGraw-Hill, 1959). See also his pamphlet, *Recommendations for Education in the Junior High School Years* (Educational Testing Service, 1960).

Proposals for substantial changes in secondary-school organization and staff utilization are presented by J. Lloyd Trump and Dorsey Baynham in *Focus on Change: A Guide to Better Schools* (Rand McNally, 1961). Attempts to make extensive changes in a school are described in B. Frank Brown's *The Nongraded High School* (Prentice-Hall, 1963).

The professional organization to which most secondary-school administrators belong is the National Association of Secondary-School Principals. Its official journal is the monthly *NASSP Bulletin*. Each volume of this periodical contains numerous articles on administrative and organizational questions. Sometimes an entire issue is devoted to such topics. The May, 1963, issue (Volume 47), for example, entitled "Changing Secondary Schools," described innovations in schools throughout the country.

## Chapter Three

# The Program of Studies

Curriculum specialists maintain that the curriculum of a school encompasses far more than its formal course offerings. They define curriculum as all the planned learning experiences that pupils have under the auspices of the school, including club meetings, assemblies, homeroom sessions, dances, ball games, and counseling interviews. When the word "planned" is omitted, as it sometimes is, the concept of curriculum becomes so broad that it includes everything a pupil does in school from which he learns anything, whether it be in the cafeteria, the corridors, or the washroom. To say that the curriculum includes experiences over which the school has little control or which it has no intention of promoting does not seem very helpful, however. And yet the point is well taken that what is actually experienced is more important than what is merely planned, whether or not the intended learning ensues.

If one distinguishes carefully between curriculum and instruction, however, it becomes clear that curriculum does not consist of experiences at all. Curriculum consists of ordered, intended learning outcomes. Deciding what experiences will produce these outcomes is instructional planning, and providing those experiences is instruction. Since these distinctions are seldom made, the prevailing notion of curriculum is that of "planned learning experiences."

OFFERINGS AND REQUIREMENTS

With the broadening of the concept of curriculum, it has become customary to refer to the organized course offerings as the *instructional program* or the *program of studies*. Nevertheless, various combinations of courses offered by a large school are commonly referred to as curriculums, each with a descriptive modifier—such as college-preparatory, general, commercial, or some other indication of emphasis or subsequent use. For the diverse student bodies found in most secondary schools, this kind of *multiple* curriculum is usually considered preferable to a *single* curriculum for all students. Indeed, there are those who feel that even six or eight course patterns are too few to provide for the numerous differences among students. A third curriculum plan, in which each student is provided with the particular combination of courses considered most appropriate for him, is perhaps the most prevalent one. It is known as the *constants-with-variables* plan.

Few American secondary schools now have a single required curriculum. Those that do are either specialized high schools for selected students or so small that no choice can be offered; or else they serve a community so homogeneous that none is necessary. As long ago as 1890 most schools offered more than one curriculum: a classical curriculum with Latin and Greek, an English curriculum with two modern languages, a scientific curriculum with one modern language, and, often, a "normal" curriculum for students who upon graduation planned to become elementary-school teachers. Nevertheless, the single curriculum still has its advocates among those who believe that specialization should be delayed and that secondary education should consist of an extended, essential, coherent general education which all students share regardless of what they may do in the future.[1]

For many years most schools provided what was virtually a single curriculum in grades seven and eight. Variables were not introduced until the ninth grade. Even so, this common instructional program was often modified into "regular," "enriched," and "adjusted" curriculums. Similar adaptation of the constants or required subjects of the higher grades increases the diversity of the curriculum even though students are given no choice among the resulting versions of these courses. Thus all curriculum variables are not electives.

There has never been much support for a completely elective secondary-school curriculum. Indeed, in order to give priority to the more essential learnings and to assure some coherence in students' programs, schools have required that students take certain subjects in order to graduate and that they also choose a major sequence representing some degree of concentration. Furthermore, not all electives are free or unrestricted; sometimes students must choose one of several specified courses. These are called limited electives.

Requirements for high-school graduation differ from state to

[1] See Harry Broudy, B. O. Smith, and Joe Burnett, *Democracy and Excellence in American Secondary Education,* Rand McNally, 1964.

state, and in some states they are left entirely to the local school system. Commonly, sixteen Carnegie units are required for graduation. A Carnegie unit consists of the study of a subject for the equivalent of 200 minutes a week for a school year, with assigned study outside class. This system of academic accounting is based entirely on the time devoted to a course, and credit is either granted in full or withheld completely, depending on whether or not the course is "passed." No allowance is made for differential quality of performance or for variations in the difficulty or value of courses.

In a number of states a distinction is made between diplomas issued by the state and diplomas issued by the local school. In New York, students must pass the well-known Regents examination in order to earn a state diploma. In addition to physical education, a total of eighteen units is required, of which four must be in English, three in social studies, one in science, one in mathematics, and a half-unit in health. Thus, prescribed courses make up about half of the requirements. In addition to these "constants," a sequence of at least three units in one of the following fields is required: science, mathematics, a foreign language, music, art, mechanical drawing, industrial arts, homemaking, agriculture, and industrial or technical subjects. For persons who for one reason or another fail to complete high school, New York awards an "equivalency diploma" on the basis of special tests of general educational development, without regard to courses completed or units amassed.

## GENERAL AND SPECIALIZED EDUCATION

Few educational concepts are more troublesome and controversial than that of general education. While it is perfectly clear that people differ and therefore presumably do not all have the same educational needs, it is also clear that people have a great deal in common, especially those who live in the same society and share the same culture. Furthermore, the first concern of every society in educating its young is to transmit its culture. Some aspects of the cultural heritage are considered so important that it is felt they ought to be shared by all members of the society. Even in a highly developed society, much of this transmission is done informally in the family and the community and by various social institutions other than the school. But the more complex the society, and therefore the more advanced the common learnings, the greater becomes the responsibility of the school to provide them. Common schooling in the United States, once limited to elementary education, now includes much if not all of secondary education.

In an "open society," widely shared learnings contribute to cohesion as well as to perpetuation. Where rigid, traditional class lines are absent, a society must have some other mechanism for maintaining cohesion. In a democracy, the sharing of knowledge, attitudes, and experiences by most of the members of the society serves as a kind of societal cement. During the decades of heavy immigration to this country, the problem of social integration was especially acute. The schools' success in "Americanization" during this period led Henry Steele Commager to declare that "our schools have kept us free."

It is easier to agree that certain learnings should be common to all than it is to agree on what those learnings should be. Some prefer that they be kept to a minimum, in order that individual differences may be fully recognized. Others advocate a common program throughout both the elementary and the secondary school.

In most schools the curriculum ostensibly retains a common component, albeit in diminishing amount, right through senior high school. Whether the existence of this component assures that common learnings ensue is not clear, however.

At one time schools expected all pupils not only to acquire the same learnings but to do so at the same rate. Thus "minimum essentials" were set for each grade, and pupils were prevented from advancing until they had mastered those essentials. When the fallaciousness of this practice became recognized, the schools stressed common *experiences* rather than the results of the experiences. Thus educators rejected the concepts of minimum essentials and adopted the view that all the school need do was to expose all pupils to the same experiences without expecting or insisting that all of them acquire any specified learning. Common learning came to mean little more than learning in common.

There is a sensible alternative to both this lack of expectation and the earlier expectation of uniform progress. In the first place, minimum essentials or common learnings should be defined quite specifically, but quite modestly. Then, while not impeding students' progress because they fail to acquire certain learnings at a particular time, schools should require each student, so long as he remains in school, to continue receiving instruction in any essential that he has not learned satisfactorily.

Although all common learnings are necessarily part of general education, not all general education consists of common learnings. General education has unique as well as common elements, an individual as well as a societal aspect. The adjective "general" refers not to the nature of the learnings but to the purpose of acquiring them. Specialization is usually aimed at the development of an extraordinary talent possessed by few or preparation for a specific vocation in which not everyone will engage. General education, on the other hand, is pursued with no specific use in mind. Its applicability is broad and unpredictable. Its outcomes, as a Harvard committee has suggested, include effective thinking, communication, the ability to make relevant judgments, and discrimination among values.[2] All *academic* study at the secondary-school level, and indeed during the first two years of college, is general education. It may not be identical for all students, including for some of them more foreign language, for others more science and mathematics, for still others more of the arts. But the goal of such study is the general one of becoming an educated person.

Educators do not agree, however, on what an educated person is. One group emphasizes familiarity with liberal studies, consisting of three categories: the natural sciences and mathematics; the social sciences and history; and the humanities, including language, philosophy, and the arts. Another group is concerned more with the functionality of learnings than with their liberality. These educators have little faith that academic learnings, widely applicable though they may be, will indeed be applied. Those who hold this view believe that the educated person is one who has been taught specifically to deal with problems of living. Their version of general education includes specific instruction in health, family living, personality development, and problems of democracy. Teachers of academic subjects are urged to emphasize these matters in their instruction if separate courses are not created to deal with them. In either case, this direct training for life should be done through learning experiences that are as lifelike as possible.

This functional view of general education is based on Edward L. Thorndike's "identical elements" theory of the transfer of learning. According to this theory the more closely the learning situation resembles the application situation, the greater is the probability that

2 Harvard Committee, *General Education in a Free Society*, Harvard University Press, 1952, p. 65.

transfer will take place. The proponents of an academic general education, on the other hand, rely more heavily on Charles H. Judd's theory that transfer depends on the acquisition of generalizations which can be applied to specific situations when appropriate. They also emphasize the importance of learning the *structure* of a discipline. A student who knows the *conceptual* structure of a subject has a framework for relating new knowledge to previously acquired knowledge. A student who knows the *syntactical* structure—the assumptions and methods appropriate to a subject—is able to judge the validity of new knowledge and estimate with what degree of confidence it may be held.

Both these theories of transfer have some validity. Teachers must help students both to develop generalizations and to recognize the practical significance of generalizations. In recent years schools have begun to give increased attention to the discovery of logical relationships among concepts and generalizations. The curriculum must be organized in a way that facilitates such discovery.

## CURRICULUM PATTERNS

Organization is an essential feature of a curriculum, whether it is for general or specialized education. A number of organizational patterns exist in secondary schools. The most common one by far is the *subject* curriculum. Other patterns have been advocated much more extensively than they have been used.

In the typical elementary school, teachers present a number of different subjects to a single grade, whereas in the secondary school they usually teach a single subject to one or more grades. When the junior high school was established, the departmentalization and subject specialization which are characteristic of secondary education were introduced into the seventh and eighth grades. But these features are not essential attributes of the subject curriculum. The curriculum can be organized by subjects whether they are taught by subject specialists or by grade specialists.

A subject may be the derivative of a scholarly discipline, of several disciplines, or of an area of practical activity that permits of being taught. A *subject* should be distinguished from a *course*. Subjects may be organized into a number of courses for instructional purposes. If the organization is done properly, the logical structure of the subject is elucidated. Faulty organization may obscure both the main ideas of the subject and the relations among them. All too often subjects have been treated as mere collections of cognate items of information to be memorized. When so viewed, they are of little value in interpreting experience.

Several decades ago dissatisfaction with the prevailing organization of subjects prompted numerous efforts to find a more suitable curriculum pattern. John Dewey's emphasis on the role of experience in learning suggested the possibility of an *experience* curriculum in the elementary school. Under this pattern, the skillful teacher makes the fortuitous everyday experiences of children rich in educative value. She contrives additional learning experiences on the basis of interests manifested by the pupils. Obviously, it is impossible to predict in advance what the interests and experiences will be or what knowledge and skills will be acquired. What is learned may be psychologically relevant but not necessarily logically related.

Relatively few schools adopted this curriculum pattern, despite the enthusiastic recommendations of many authorities on elementary education from about 1915 to the 1940's. These leaders seemed to consider the informal, phenomenological manner in which illiterate preschool children learn to be a more "natural," and hence better, way of learning than learning through logically organized subjects. This argument has some validity for the early years of the elementary school, when a child's cognitive structure is rudimentary and when he can relate new learnings only to what is familiar in his own experience. Although it is desirable at all levels for students to relate abstract learning to reality whenever possible, the function of the curriculum is to create artificial learning situations which produce an organization of knowledge that does not ensue from ordinary experiences. Moreover, as children grow, their interests and experiences differ so greatly that they offer little basis for organizing the curriculum. The experience curriculum, therefore, has had little influence on secondary education.

Under a somewhat related plan, known as the *activity* curriculum, logically organized subjects were replaced by planned activities and projects from which pupils would simultaneously acquire learnings based on several fields of knowledge. This approach emphasized "doing" rather than learning. It based motivation more on the students' interest in completing a particular task or project than on their desire to acquire the intended learning. It also tried to "integrate" learnings that would otherwise be compartmentalized by subject. The use of activities to supplement subject instruction in the elementary school is not uncommon, and even at the lower secondary-school level teachers use activities as a means of clarifying concepts and applying skills within subjects. But the agitation for integration has presented the single most insistent challenge to the integrity of subjects in the secondary-school curriculum.

The term integration has been used to mean many things in education. It is, of course, applied in race relations as a synonym for desegregation. In addition, it is used in a psychological sense to mean the incorporation of a number of individual responses into coordinated action, and in a mental-health context to imply a whole-some consistency of personality. As a function of schools, integration denotes the unifying role of general education in a society. In discussions of curriculum and instruction, however, integration can mean either the synthesizing of previously acquired learnings into larger meanings or functional behavior patterns, or the actual blending of two or more subjects of study.

In this last sense, integration is to be distinguished from "correlation," in which teachers, either independently or by agreement, emphasize the legitimate relationships between subjects while preserving the demarcations between them. A conscientious teacher explicates such relationships whenever possible. For two teachers to agree on an arrangement of their subjects that will facilitate correlation between them requires much initiative and entails some risk. The organization of both subjects may become so distorted that more is lost than gained. To select literature for English classes on the basis of what students are studying in history is to misconstrue the purposes of studying literature, and to interrupt the study of history in order to teach the principles of English grammar may destroy the continuity on which both motivation and understanding depend. Yet some curriculum specialists have advocated that correlation be carried to the point of organizing all or most of the required subjects for each grade around some all-encompassing theme for the year.

Whether it is desirable or not, this degree of correlation is extremely difficult to achieve. That may be why, during the late 1930's, the proponents of integration suggested that the demarcations between subjects were artificial and that only by completely unifying two or more subjects could integrated learning be realized. "Unified studies" scheduled for a "block of time" consisting of two or three consecutive periods are not uncommon in junior high schools. Sometimes known as "general education," "common learnings," or "core," these courses usually combine English and social studies. Often the teacher is responsible as well for the personal guidance of students— a task that may otherwise be the responsibility of a homeroom teacher. In many instances, even in a unified-studies situation, the two subjects are taught separately, albeit by the same teacher. When they are actually unified, the social studies usually provide the organizing framework into which the English learnings are woven. Whether or not the subjects are actually unified, the teacher is ordinarily a specialist in only one or the other of them. To the objection that he is, therefore, not really qualified to teach the other subject, enthusiasts for the unified-studies plan argue that if one teacher can teach all subjects in grade six, he can teach at least two in grade seven. Furthermore, by having the pupils for more than one period he can get to know them and their needs better and can ease their transition to complete departmentalization.

Under the unified-studies plan the logical organization of at least one of the combined subjects is usually retained. In what is known as a "true core program," however, neither English nor social studies is taught as such. Instead, students "solve problems" by "drawing upon" these and other subjects for their data. Problem-solving can and should take place in the course of studying any subject, but advocates of the core curriculum point out that "real life" problems do not fall neatly within the bounds of a single subject. If students are to learn to solve problems, they must deal with problems that are real to them. In the philosophy of core these include the personal problems students experience in the course of growing up and the pressing current social problems that they read about and hear discussed.

One may object that the personal problems are too trivial and transitory to warrant valuable instructional time, and that the social problems are so complex that without a great deal of further systematic learning young pupils cannot even comprehend, let alone solve, them. But to these demurrers, supporters of the core program reply that the test of a free man is not the formal knowledge he possesses but his ability to cope independently and rationally with the problems of living, and that the mark of a democratic citizen is not what he knows about democracy but the effectiveness with which he joins in the collective solution of social problems.

What is more, some advocates of core insist that pupils should not only learn to "solve" problems cooperatively but that they should have the opportunity to identify the problems and reach agreement on which ones they will tackle. In such an *unstructured* core, the teacher is deprived of any course of study and must rely only on some agreed-upon criteria and his own judgment in guiding his class in the selection of what they will study. In the more moderate *structured* core program, the members of the faculty agree beforehand on what problems are to be included in each grade's program. Beyond this stipulation, however, the only structure for learning is the rather stereotyped procedure used in cooperative problem-solving. But this structure is as good as any, say the supporters of core, so long as scholars are unable to identify a single inherent structure for each discipline.

The core curriculum first attracted attention as a result of the "Eight-Year Study" of the 1930's. In this study 30 schools tried various departures from the traditional subject organization and found that the success of students in college does not depend on their having followed a particular pattern of courses in high school.[3] The core pattern achieved its greatest popularity during the early 1950's. Its use declined with the growing interest in systematic intellectual development that came with the early space explorations toward the end of the decade. Most existing core programs are found at the junior-high-school level and consist essentially of English and social studies taught in a two-period "block of time."

Most experimental studies show that pupils taught in a core program do as well on standarized achievement tests as comparable students who studied separate subjects.[4] These findings may indicate that the core programs did not actually depart radically from subject teaching and that only quite skillful teachers were willing to attempt core teaching. They may also indicate that what is emphasized in conventional subject teaching and measured by conventional achievement tests does not truly reflect a disciplinary structure. Criticisms of the core-curriculum idea apply equally to subjects which consist of poorly organized compendia of inert facts.

The subject curriculum seems destined to survive as the chief pattern for organizing instruction in the secondary school. Many so-

---

[3] Wilford Aiken, *The Story of the Eight-Year Study*, Harper & Row, 1942.
[4] Grace Wright, *The Core Program, Abstracts of Unpublished Research: 1946–1955*, U.S. Office of Education, 1956, p. 14.

called subjects are, however, actually *fusions* of component subjects. Social studies, English, and biology are obvious examples. Other *broad fields* or survey courses, such as general science and introduction to business, include an even greater variety of specific subjects. Thus, *within* fields there is much integration of the sort the core plan seeks to effect *between* fields.

A teacher who is a "specialist" in a secondary-school subject is expected to have a strong preparation in a much wider area of study than is expected of a specialist at the college level. The difficulty of achieving such extensive mastery and of keeping abreast of change argues against any further combination of subjects in the secondary-school curriculum. Indeed, it may even suggest the desirability of dividing some current offerings into more homogeneous and specialized courses in which a more logical and coherent structure might be made explicit. Secondary-school students need to have teachers who are masters of the subjects they teach. The curriculum organization should not force teachers to profess greater mastery than they possess.

*Suggestions for Class Discussion and Further Investigation*

1. How much freedom should secondary-school students be permitted in choosing courses? Is the current diversification of offerings justified? Would it be better to offer a limited number of subjects and require all students to take them, but at different paces and to different levels of accomplishment?

2. What are the advantages and disadvantages of the Carnegie unit (as an academic measure)? Can you think of a better system? Should all subjects be counted as of equal value? Should quality of performance be considered? Should "enriched" or honor courses count the same as "regular" ones? Would a comprehensive examination be preferable to any system of credit counting?

3. What should general education for all normal citizens consist of?

4. What are the advantages of teaching subjects separately and by specialists? What advantages do you see in forgetting about distinctions among subjects? Do personal and societal problems offer a good basis for organizing a curriculum?

5. What differences, if any, between secondary education in urban and rural areas can be justified?

*Suggestions for Further Reading*

Two bulletins issued by the U.S. Office of Education provide data on the programs of studies of American high schools. These are *What High School Pupils Study,* by Edith S. Greer and Richard M. Harbeck (Office of Education Bulletin 1962, No. 10, Government Printing Office, 1962), and Grace S. Wright's *Requirements for High School Graduation* (Office of Education Bulletin 1961, No. 12, Government Printing Office, 1961). A convenient source of information about the Carnegie unit is an article by Ellsworth Tompkins and Walter Gaumnitz, "The Carnegie Unit: Its Origin, Status, and Trends," in the *Bulletin of the National Association of Secondary School Principals,* 48 (January, 1964), pp. 1–78.

The professional organization most concerned with the curriculum as a whole is the Association for Supervision and Curriculum Development (ASCD). The Association's yearbook for 1956, entitled *What Shall the High Schools Teach?,* contained a chapter by Kenneth Hovet which answered, for that pre-Sputnik year, the question, "What *Are* the High Schools Teaching?" (pp. 69–96). Two other chapters of interest to the student of the high-school curriculum are Lawrence A. Cremin's "The Problem of Curriculum Making: An Historical Perspective" (pp. 6–26), and Arno A. Bellack's "Selection and Organization of Curriculum Content: An Analysis" (pp. 97–106).

The problem of general versus special education is also treated in the 1956 *ASCD Yearbook.* Some of the many interpretations of general education are enumerated by George H. Henry in a chapter entitled "Foundations of General Education in the High School" (pp. 127–75), and some definitions are offered by James E. Spitznas in "General, Special and Vocational Education: An Exploration of Distinctive Differences" (pp. 176–211). For a view of general education by a group of scholars keenly aware of the dual need for unity and diversity in society, see the Harvard Committee's Report, *General Education in a Free Society* (Harvard University Press, 1952). Two chapters are especially relevant: "Theory of General Education" (pp. 42–78), and "Areas of General Education: The Secondary Schools" (pp. 103–76).

Representative of thinking about the curriculum prior to the reform movement is Harold B. Alberty's book, *Reorganizing the High-School Curriculum* (Macmillan, 1949). Alberty identifies six conceptions of core curriculum, four of which are used by Grace S. Wright in her study of *Core Curriculum Development, Problems and Practices* (Office of Education Bulletin 1952, No. 5, Government Printing Office, 1952). A more thorough treatment of this curriculum form is to be found in *Developing the Core Curriculum,* 2nd ed., by Roland C. Faunce and Nelson L. Bossing (Prentice-Hall, 1958).

A brief summary and critical assessment of more recent curriculum developments is provided by John I. Goodlad in *School Curriculum Reform* (Fund for the Advancement of Education, 1964). Philip H. Phenix, in his *Realms of Meaning* (McGraw-Hill, 1964), has identified six types of meaning for which provision must be made in the curriculum. The main part of Phenix's book is devoted to the key concepts and structural bases of the various disciplines. Joseph J. Schwab also deals with "The Structure of the Disciplines" in the first chapter of *The Structure of Knowledge and the Curriculum,* G. W. Ford and Lawrence Pugno, eds. (Rand McNally, 1964). Hollis L. Caswell, an early leader in the field of curriculum who later became president of Teachers College, Columbia University, discusses "Difficulties in Defining the Structure of the Curriculum" on pages 103–11 of *Curriculum Crossroads,* edited by A. Harry Passow.

One of several volumes produced by the National Education Association's Project on Instruction offers recommendations for improving the curriculum. The content of this volume, *Deciding What To Teach,* by Dorothy M. Fraser (National Education Association, 1963), may also be found in condensed form as a chapter in *Schools for the Sixties* (National Education Association, 1963), pp. 27–62.

*Chapter Four*

# The Academic Subjects

Some educators object to the practice of labeling certain subjects "academic" and others "nonacademic." They argue that such a distinction is invalid and that it introduces a false connotation of prestige. Nevertheless, the distinction is widely recognized, and it is based on the nature and source of the subjects, not on their prestige. The academic subjects derive from the scholarly disciplines, whereas other subjects stem from the various fields of man's practical activity.

The study of language, number, nature, art, man, and society is fundamental to many other kinds of study and to most human enterprises. Moreover, the intellectual component of these studies exceeds that of other studies. While these subjects are commonly called academic, they are in a sense the most practical of all studies, because their usefulness is not limited to any specific kind of activity.

### ENGLISH

English is almost universally required in each of the six secondary-school years. Embracing the study of both the language and the literature, the subject is a fusion of many components that were once taught separately: reading, grammar, orthography, elocution, rhetoric, forensics, composition, literature, criticism. Paradoxically, although English teachers are on the whole more thoroughly prepared in literature than in composition, the recent tendency in defining the study has been to reduce it to the acquisition of four "tools"—the so-called language arts or communication skills of reading, writing, speaking, and listening.

Ostensibly, the teacher of English has an advantage over his colleagues, for his subject is practiced by students in their every waking hour and is applied in every course they take. In reality, however, he labors feebly against the powerful reinforcing effects of the speech patterns of family and street, against the dearth of good reading material in the home, against the influence of television and movies, and, often, against an indifference toward proper usage on the part of other teachers. To make matters worse, controversies abound regarding the purposes and procedures of teaching English. If English teachers feel frustrated, they can hardly be blamed.

For many years the teaching of formal grammar has been challenged by those who favor teaching grammatical principles either not at all, or incidentally as errors repeatedly arise in students' writing. Actually, there are several issues: whether rules and analysis help writing at all, whether rules should be learned systematically or only in a functional setting, and whether grammar is prescriptive or descriptive. Recently, some linguistic scientists have raised another issue by suggesting that a scientific, descriptive approach to the analysis of language is preferable to the study of traditional grammar. This controversy goes on in colleges and universities as well as in secondary schools, and it will be many years before it is resolved. Meanwhile, the high-school English teacher must keep informed of the arguments, study linguistics, try new approaches, and make professional decisions on what approach or combination of approaches to use.

There is rather general agreement that increased attention should be given to students' writing, that students should write frequently, and that English teachers cannot be assigned more than a hundred students if they are to teach this skill successfully. There is less agreement on whether, and how, laymen should be employed to assist the teacher in reading students' papers. Some schools employ "composition aides" instead of reducing the load of English teachers; a few do both. The majority of schools do neither.

Also at issue are the place of reading instruction in the secondary-school English program and the respective roles of English teachers, other teachers, and reading specialists in that instruction. Regular instruction in reading was commonly provided in grades seven and eight when those grades were part of the elementary school. The need for such instruction did not, of course, disappear when those grades were incorporated into the secondary school. Indeed, it became increasingly apparent that reading is an extremely complex process in which most students continue to develop throughout high school. Many students who, in an earlier era, would never have reached high school now enter it without enough proficiency in reading to perform the tasks required of them. Thus the importance of both a developmental and a remedial approach to reading throughout the secondary school has become widely recognized.

Remedial instruction calls for a specialist's talents, and the teaching of specialized study techniques and technical vocabulary are the responsibility of each subject teacher. But the main burden of the developmental reading program falls on English teachers, many of whom have no preparation for teaching reading even though reading is usually considered the most important of the four language arts.

Speech specialists, too, are seldom pleased with the manner in which speech is dealt with in English classes. Emphasis has shifted from formal oral presentations to more informal discussion, conversation, and even telephone procedure. The specialists themselves tend to emphasize different aspects. Some of them stress discussion skills, others stress speech mechanics; some emphasize rhetoric and public address, others lay stress on drama and dramatic interpretation. Obviously, each of these aspects can receive but little attention in English courses, which must deal not only with language but with literature as well.

Despite the fact that most English teachers are best prepared in literature, problems abound in the teaching of literature, too. New teachers are often dissatisfied with the selections imposed on them by curriculum outlines or by the anthologies available in the school. Still, if none were required, it would be difficult for them to find selections that either all or none of the students in a class had already read. But a more serious difficulty is that unless the class is fairly homogeneous in reading ability, no selection, required or not, will be appropriate for all to read. Some teachers, therefore, in an effort to ensure class discussion, use several books of varying difficulty but on similar themes, on the assumption that it is the theme or the substance of a work that is of greatest importance.

Actually, there is no universal agreement on the purposes of studying literature. Some teachers emphasize well-known passages and the specific details of plots, characters, and authors' lives, apparently to make students well informed *about* literature. Some stress the ideas and universal truths that are dealt with, the goal being to learn *from* literature. Others strive to have students solve their own personal problems through a kind of biblio-therapy in which they identify with characters in situations similar to their own. Still others emphasize form and style rather than content, seeking to develop esthetic tastes and an understanding of the principles of literary criticism.

The organization of the course and the selection of readings are both related to purpose. If form is of primary concern, the organization is often historical or by genre, and the selections are chosen mainly from standard adult literature, with perhaps some mediocre juvenile literature for contrast. If content is regarded as most important, the study is organized around broad themes or so-called centers of interest, and much use is made of contemporary material written for, and often about, young people. Although much of this kind of writing is of poor quality, if not trashy, a teacher who knows children's literature can find worthwhile reading that has meaning for younger or less able students. Nevertheless, students will be deprived of their literary heritage if they are not brought into contact with as many authors of acknowledged quality as possible.

Scholars do not agree, nor can they be expected to agree, on any list of selections that *must* be read, even by students planning to attend college. Most English teachers are or should be aware of what is good literature, and students during their secondary-school years should be encouraged and aided to read critically as much of it as they can. It is sound pedagogy to capitalize on students' interests, but interests mature, and new ones can be developed. High-school seniors should be mature enough to be able to read both classics and contemporary adult material, although many communities do not consider the language and subject matter of much contemporary writing suitable for classroom study by mixed groups.

There is so much great literature and even more that is good that it seems a pity for high-school students to spend time on selections that are neither. Students are entitled to help in learning what is considered excellent and should be encouraged to read extensively beyond what they study in class. The teacher of literature teaches how to read, as well as how one *should* read, and what is worth reading. He also stimulates students *to* read and to want to keep on reading.

## MATHEMATICS

Although one of the effects of the reorganization movement in secondary education was to introduce algebra and geometry topics into grades seven and eight, the mathematics in those grades is still largely arithmetic. Great emphasis is placed on applying the arithmetic already learned to a variety of practical situations, mostly relating to business. In many instances the only new arithmetic topics introduced are percentage and proportion.

Elementary algebra has traditionally been offered in the ninth grade. Many schools, however, offer some sort of general mathematics for ninth-graders who are not ready for algebra; for many students this is the terminal course in mathematics. On the other hand, more and more schools are now offering algebra to the most able students in the eighth grade, followed by geometry or a second algebra course in the ninth.

The most significant development in the mathematics curriculum, however, is the introduction of a great deal of modern material that students hitherto did not encounter until they had reached advanced college courses. A number of revisions, such as those of the School Mathematics Study Group (SMSG), the Madison Plan, and several programs developed at the University of Illinois, emphasize the structure of mathematics and the active discovery of principles and solution methods by pupils. At ease with terminology strange to the ears of their elders, junior-high-school pupils use the concepts of set theory rather than the familiar algorithms in solving problems, and they become aware not only of the interrelationships among branches of mathematics but of the specific universes of discourse within which various operations are applicable. Thus the better students, at least, continue to advance mathematically during the junior-high-school years instead of marking time with innumerable practical applications of elementary processes. As these programs become established, many students will, by the time they leave high school, have completed analytic geometry, as well as advanced algebra and trigonometry, and often an introduction to calculus, statistics, or computer mathematics.

In mathematics, unlike English, the courses and their sequence are relatively well defined. Thus, through the acceleration of the program and the introduction of modern mathematical content, the secondary school has been able to provide the better students with a challenging and up-to-date curriculum. But again unlike English, mathematics is not usually required in the senior high school. If mathematics departments had to provide a worthwhile program for all students through the twelfth grade, some formidable problems would undoubtedly be encountered. Yet the importance of mathematics in a technological world might argue strongly for such a program. Even if additional mathematics is not required, however, many more students may elect to pursue the subject further when the courses that are required are invested with greater meaning for them. Mathematics is far more interesting as a system of thought than as a tool for routine calculations in practical applications.

## SCIENCE

The secondary-school science program is influenced greatly by two factors: the secondary-school mathematics program and the elementary-school science program. Strengthening the elementary-school science program makes it possible to move back to the junior high school much of the content of the separate courses in biology, physics, and chemistry from the senior-high years, thus permitting more rigorous courses in those later years. Without the use of more advanced mathematics than most high-school students currently acquire, however, the degree of rigor possible in the science curriculum is severely limited. This poses a dilemma, and some scientists go so far as to suggest limiting high-school science to students who do not intend to become scientists, while increasing mathematics study for those with scientific goals.

Other scientists have created new courses which are rapidly being introduced throughout the country. Notable among these are the three-version course of the Biological Sciences Curriculum Study (BSCS), the physics course of the Physical Sciences Study Committee (PSSC), and the Chemical Education Material Study (CHEMStudy) and Chemical Bond Approach (CBA) courses in chemistry, all sponsored by the National Science Foundation. The course materials in these programs include textbooks, films showing complex experiments, and laboratory manuals outlining "open-ended" experiments, many of which students can perform with relatively simple equipment. The emphasis is on theory rather than on facts, and on genuine experimentation rather than on mere manipulation. Although future scientists may need more thorough grounding than these courses provide, they are eminently suitable for general education for nonscientists, who should understand the fundamental concepts and methods of scientific inquiry. It is a fact, however, that these courses are beyond the ability of some high-school students to understand. For the latter students, some schools have developed "second-track" courses in the biological and physical sciences at the senior-high-school level.

Where such courses are lacking, many students terminate their study of science in grade nine with the well-known general science course, which was introduced around 1915. For many years science was taught, if at all, only the equivalent of two or three periods a week in grades seven and eight. Increasingly, however, full-time study of the subject is being required in these grades. For the most part the junior-high-school courses are still general and are still organized around phenomena rather than disciplinary structures, although there are some indications that an organization into separate biological and physical sciences may come about in time. Most teachers are more thoroughly prepared either in biological or in physical science and consequently are at a disadvantage when they are required to teach a whole course in general science. For the more able students, the ninth-grade general-science course is commonly being replaced by a course in biology or earth science. Not until separate courses based on disciplinary structures are adapted to different ability levels will large numbers of secondary-school students be able to reach the level of scientific understanding that the times demand.

## SOCIAL STUDIES

The curriculum in social studies is less standard than the curriculum in either mathematics or science, and many unresolved problems exist. One of them concerns the emphasis to be placed on the several social sciences in relation to that given to the humanistic study of history. For many years history, particularly that of the United States and western Europe, has received the greatest attention, although efforts have been made to relate economics, geography, sociology, anthropology, and political science to the study of both history and current affairs. Part of the problem lies in the tremendous amount of material available in a subject that involves so many disciplines, encompasses the whole world, and covers the entire span of time from the very beginnings of man to the appearance of the morning's headlines. Superficiality has been the inevitable result, even with the virtual neglect of such large and important non-western countries as China, India, and Russia, not to mention the smaller yet increasingly significant developing nations.

Some states require that an entire year be devoted to the study of state and local matters, often in a manner that lifts them out of the context of national affairs, thus inviting charges of both imbalance and parochialism. The study of American history, required by almost every state, may occupy as many as three of the six secondary-school years. Often the treatment is repetitious, although some carefully planned programs avoid redundancy through the use, for example, of a chronological narrative approach in junior high school and a thematic or problems approach in senior high school.

It is extremely difficult to devise an appropriate structure for the social studies. The component disciplines are not only numerous but disparate. Some advocate a historical framework, with separate courses in the senior year in economics, sociology, and other social sciences. Others argue that students find more meaning in history if they first understand the concepts and methods of the social sciences. In either case, there is the problem of how to handle "current events" or "contemporary affairs," which, though often treated in isolation, are being increasingly incorporated into a planned program as a point of departure or as a source of vivid illustrations.

One deterrent to the development of a sound curriculum has been the tendency to view social studies more as an instrument for the promotion of "citizenship" and for the development of "personality" than as an intellectual enterprise. Social-studies teachers have been encouraged to make extensive use of cooperative classroom activities, such as "committee work" and "group problem solving." By sharing and discussing data collected independently, students are expected to reach consensus on matters ranging from absurdly trivial personal problems to inordinately complex social issues. This approach to social studies reflects greater concern with experience in the democratic process than with the organized knowledge and the sense of history that the individual needs in order to function as an enlightened citizen in a free society. Somewhere in its total program, the school should give students opportunities to practice democratic skills and to get help with personal problems. But organizing social studies for these purposes obscures the structure of both history and the social sciences.

FOREIGN LANGUAGES

The influence of goals upon program content and instructional methods is also evident in the teaching of foreign languages. When reading and writing were the primary goals, the emphasis was on learning grammatical forms and rules. The study of a modern language was usually preceded by Latin, which was not offered until grade nine. Students commonly studied one language for three years or two languages for two years. Between 1905 and 1955, the percentage of students studying Latin dropped from 50 to 7, and for modern languages the decrease was from 29 to 14 per cent. When speaking fluency and oral comprehension became important goals, it became evident that modern-language instruction could and should begin much earlier than the ninth grade, that it should be largely conversational at the outset, and that Latin need no longer be the first language studied. Ideally, oral-aural (or audio-lingual) language instruction should begin in the elementary school at around the fourth grade, before pupils become inhibited by self-consciousness and fixed speech habits. The amount of instruction in foreign languages in the elementary school (called FLES, for short) increased greatly in the late 1950's and early 1960's. Nevertheless, the scarcity of qualified teachers, the unavailability of funds, and the lack of consensus on the desirability of such instruction at this level have conspired to limit the program to a minority of systems. In most systems, therefore, foreign-language instruction still begins in the secondary school, though increasingly in the seventh grade rather than in the ninth.

The federal funds made available by the National Defense Education Act of 1958 enabled many teachers to receive language training at special summer and year-long institutes and helped schools to obtain tape-recording and play-back equipment for language laboratories. There was some expectation that these laboratories would constitute the chief, if not the sole, vehicle for instruction, but they have proved useful mainly in supplementing classroom instruction by providing students with opportunities to hear native pronunciation and to practice their own pronunciation. The greatest asset of any language program is a teacher who has acquired fluency, preferably through living abroad.

The provision of financial support by the federal government suggests that the national interest is served by the expansion and improvement of language instruction in the schools. If this policy is to be carried out, long-standing indifference and even resistance must be overcome. For years an isolationist sentiment, a distrust of foreigners, and an eagerness to "Americanize" immigrants generated apathy or downright hostility toward foreign-language instruction. Attitudes have changed as the result of improved communication and transportation, the overseas wartime experiences of many Americans, and the assumption of international leadership by the United

States. Still, it is widely held that, since English is rapidly becoming a world-wide language, Americans need not learn another. It is also argued that, despite its greater prevalency, the precise location of foreign service and travel is unpredictable, and hence it is fruitless to study any language but one's own in school.

Even those who grant the desirability of foreign-language study do not always agree on which languages secondary schools should offer. The decision is most critical in schools that can offer only one or two. As enrollments increase, particularly in language classes, schools can offer five or six languages and satisfy more people. In one sense, however, the problem is then shifted to the students, who must decide for themselves which languages to study.

In bilingual sections of the country it is clearly desirable to offer the language with which many students have experience at home. In the belief that such cultural ties should be preserved, Italian and Hebrew are offered in New York City, German and Scandinavian languages in the Midwest, Spanish along the Mexican border, and French near Quebec. The influx of American citizens from Puerto Rico and of refugees from Cuba increased Spanish teaching in the Northeast and Florida during the 1950's and 1960's.

Where bilingualism is not a factor, tradition and the availability of teachers often determine what is offered. French, once the language of diplomacy and therefore in a sense universal, has always been a common offering. The fact that French and German are the traditional languages of advanced scholarship is in some communities a strong argument for their inclusion in the secondary-school program. Spanish gains some popularity from its reputation for being easier to learn than the others. Some believe that the publicity given the "Good Neighbor Policy" during the 1930's may also have contributed to the displacement of French by Spanish as the most popular language. French had itself taken over first place from German in 1918, when the latter virtually disappeared from the curriculum overnight.

Thus events abroad affect the language curriculum. In the light of the current international situation, strong arguments can be advanced for the teaching of Russian and Chinese. The scarcity of qualified teachers and the difficulty of these languages greatly inhibit their entry into the curriculum, however.

Perhaps the choice of language is not really so important. Language experts claim that learning one foreign language makes learning a second one easier. What really matters, therefore, is that whatever language is offered be well taught and be studied for more than two or three years. However, since reading is a major activity in the advanced courses, a suitable language will be one in which there is a substantial body of good literature.

Although a student does not have to be highly intelligent in order to learn to speak a language, his mental ability does affect the *rate* at which he learns. Above-average intelligence seems essential to the mastery of the structural elements of a language and the achievement of literacy in it. Bright students can learn much about their own language from studying another, but whether those who are having difficulty with English should take a foreign language is questionable. Additional attention to English might be preferable. Nevertheless, it seems certain that in the future many more secondary-school students will study more foreign language than in the past.

## THE FINE ARTS

In the curriculum of most comprehensive high schools the fine arts have only a minor place. Students encounter some poetry and drama in English and foreign-language courses, and possibly some forms of the dance in physical education. Brief courses in general music and art may be required in the junior high school, but thereafter these subjects are usually elective, pursued mainly by talented students who specialize in one of the arts. Large cities may even have a separate high school of music and art or of the performing arts. But few secondary schools make a serious effort to cultivate artistic understanding and esthetic appreciation among students generally.

Secondary-school programs in the arts emphasize participation, expression, and the acquisition of facts. Participation takes place largely in a variety of extra-class performing groups, such as bands, orchestras, choruses, and dramatic clubs, for some of which academic credit may be granted. Participation in group singing is a common activity in junior-high-school general music classes. Similarly, general art courses commonly stress self-expression through a variety of media. In both music and art courses, as in the study of literature, mere memorization of specific facts about artists, works of art, and techniques may be the dominant intellectual activity.

There is nothing wrong with any of these activities in themselves. Performance probably enhances appreciation. For some students it may lead to a pleasurable leisure pursuit. Creative self-expression contributes to the acquisition of esthetic meanings. But self-expression without the discipline of technique is more indulgent than enlightening. And except for the few students with genuine talent, participation is likely to be limited to popular art forms, and no amount of such participation can increase awareness and understanding of serious music or art. Nor is there any reason to believe that memorization cultivates taste.

Yet the secondary school ought to strive to increase artistic sophistication and elevate esthetic tastes. Students do not need exposure to what is popular; their environment is saturated with it. The school should provide them with bases for criticizing common art forms and for recognizing excellence in music, painting, sculpture, architecture, poetry, and other esthetic areas. High-fidelity recording and color photography make it technically possible to bring reproductions of the finest artistic achievements into the classroom. The focus of attention in esthetics is the specific work of art. Unless students' lives are to be devoid of significant esthetic meanings, they must encounter examples of serious art in school and learn how to derive meaning from them. They should know what to listen for at a concert and what to look for in an art museum. Just as they should learn how a scientist or a historian works or how a mathematician thinks, they should learn how an artist perceives a piece of art.

Broudy and his associates have suggested that ". . . the area of the curriculum primarily responsible for conveying to the pupil a sense of the style or styles of life found admirable by the connoisseurs of our culture should consist of six years of study devoted to a carefully selected set of paintings, musical compositions, poems, dramas, and novels."[1] These selections they call "exemplars." Extending serious study of the arts throughout the secondary-school years offers the possibility of developing "cultured masses" who will reject the "mass culture" that too few deplore today.

## Suggestions for Class Discussion and Further Investigation

1. Examine the subject area in which you are most thoroughly prepared for alternative logical structures. Identify its domain of concern, its most fundamental assumptions, the methods by

---

[1] Harry S. Broudy, B. Othanel Smith, and Joe R. Burnett, *Democracy and Excellence in American Secondary Education,* Rand McNally, 1964, p. 229.

which inquiry is carried out, and the most central concepts with which it deals.

2. Discuss the relevance of humanistic studies in contemporary society and suggest ways in which a coherent approach to the humanities might be achieved in the six-year secondary school.

3. It is usually easier to reach agreement on the importance of studying English, history, mathematics, and science than on the importance of studying foreign languages. How do you account for this? Should not everyone study foreign languages? If not, who should?

## Suggestions for Further Reading

For each subject, numerous "methods" books discuss the content of courses, objectives, and differing views on proper emphases, in addition to teaching techniques. The professional societies in each subject issue journals and, in some cases, yearbooks. Each teacher should know these sources well for his own field.

Familiarity with new courses developed by national curriculum groups is best achieved by examining the actual materials produced by these groups. Several books summarize the work of these committees—for example, *New Curricula,* edited by Robert W. Heath (Harper & Row, 1964), *Modern Viewpoints in the Curriculum,* edited by Paul Rosenbloom (McGraw-Hill, 1964), and *Current Curriculum Studies in Academic Subjects* by Dorothy M. Fraser (National Education Association, 1962). An article on "The New Curricula" by Evans Clinchy is included in *The Revolution in the Schools,* edited by Ronald Gross and Judith Murphy (Harcourt, Brace & World, 1964), pp. 220–40. A report of a disciplines seminar sponsored by the N.E.A. Project on Instruction is also of interest. Entitled *The Scholars Look at the Schools,* it was prepared by Dorsey Baynham (National Education Association, 1962).

Another seminar, sponsored by Phi Delta Kappa, dealt with the structure of knowledge in the various academic subjects. The report, *Education and the Structure of Knowledge,* was edited by Stanley Elam (Rand McNally, 1964). Harry S. Broudy discusses the arts (pp. 75–120); Norwood Russell Hanson, the physical sciences (pp. 148–87); and William Oliver Martin, the social sciences (pp. 188–220). A summary chapter by Arno A. Bellack,

"Knowledge Structure and the Curriculum" (pp. 263–77), considers the problems of relating instruction to human affairs and taking into account the psychological order of development when the curriculum is organized in accordance with disciplinary structures.

The views of a number of scholars who conducted a study of secondary education in Portland, Oregon, are presented in a volume by Albert R. Kitzhaber, Robert M. Gorrell, and Paul Roberts entitled *Education for College* (Ronald, 1961). For reactions of school administrators to the ferment in curriculum, see the issue of the *Bulletin of the National Association of Secondary-School Principals* (Vol. 47, November, 1963) that was devoted to "Secondary-School Curricular Areas: Issues and Developments."

New publications are appearing regularly in every subject field. They may be historical, such as Donald E. Stahl's *A History of the English Curriculum in American High Schools* (Lyceum Press, 1965), or visionary, such as *Goals for School Mathematics,* the report of the Cambridge Conference on School Mathematics (Educational Services Incorporated, 1963). Each one brings new insights on the secondary-school curriculum. Some present the thinking of scholars regarding the teaching of their disciplines in the schools—for example, *The Social Studies and the Social Sciences,* jointly sponsored by the American Council of Learned Societies and the National Council for the Social Studies (Harcourt, Brace & World, 1962); and Erling M. Hunt, *et al., High School Social Studies Perspectives* (Houghton Mifflin, 1962).

The final report of the Commission on English (Harold C. Martin, Chairman), entitled *Freedom and Discipline in English* (College Entrance Examination Board, 1965), is well worth reading by any secondary-school teacher and mandatory for teachers of English.

## Chapter Five

# Practical Subjects

Since the Latin grammar schools of colonial times taught only classical studies, private entrepreneurs found it profitable to offer instruction in various practical subjects needed by the people. When Benjamin Franklin proposed the first academy, he wanted its curriculum to include these subjects, along with such "academic" studies as English, mathematics, and science, which were not part of the classical program. Recognizing that art is long and students' time is short, he felt that only those things "that are likely to be most useful and most ornamental" should be taught.

In the middle of the eighteenth century the economy was predominantly agrarian, but maritime trade was expanding, domestic commerce was growing, and the frontier was advancing. Accordingly, the most useful subjects were agriculture, navigation, bookkeeping, and surveying. These were utilitarian subjects with an intellectual basis. Franklin did not suggest that the skilled trades be taught in school; these were to be learned through indentured apprenticeships, as he himself had learned printing.

Although that first academy tended to neglect the "useful" subjects in favor of the ornamental classics, many of those that came after it provided both kinds of instruction. Moreover, the purpose of the first high school, established in 1821, was ". . . to qualify a youth to fill usefully and respectably many of those stations both public and private, in which he may be placed . . ." and to provide ". . . an education that shall fit him for active life, and shall serve as a foundation for eminence in his profession, whether mercantile or mechanical. . . ."[1] First in the academies and then in the high schools, the dual aim of training students for life and preparing them for college has characterized American secondary education since the founding of the nation.

[1] Emit D. Grizzell, *Origin and Development of the High School in New England Before 1865*, Macmillan, 1923, p. 277.

66

In 1917 the first federal legislation was enacted giving financial support for vocational education in secondary schools. The Smith-Hughes Act of that year did for the high schools what the Morrill Act had done for higher education a half-century earlier by requiring the teaching of the mechanic arts and agriculture in the land-grant colleges established under its provisions. Federal support for one group of subjects may be viewed as a lack of support for others. In 1918 the "cardinal objectives" of secondary education included "vocation" but made no reference to intellectual goals beyond the so-called "fundamental processes." In 1944 "saleable skills" led all the rest of the "imperative educational needs" which "education for all American youth" was supposed to serve.

By the early 1950's, even with the nuclear era under way and with advancing scholarship and technology placing a high premium on intellectual attainment, the U.S. Office of Education was promoting a national "life adjustment" movement with an emphasis on direct training not only for vocation but for all other phases of daily life. Learnings of immediate, though limited, utility were preferred over those of potentially wider, but unpredictable, applicability.

When, toward the end of the decade, spectacular accomplishments in the exploration of space made it apparent that the security of the nation depended upon the fullest development of its intellectual resources, the federal government appropriated money for the improvement of instruction in mathematics, science, and foreign languages. Nevertheless, the National Defense Education Act of 1958 was not intended to promote the general diffusion of knowledge but rather to increase as rapidly as possible the nation's supply of engineers, mathematicians, interpreters, and other needed specialists. It was, in effect, a vocational-education measure aimed at a somewhat higher occupational level than usual. Not only did it neglect the humanities and the social sciences, but it provided specific aid for guidance services, presumably so that qualified students would be directed into the critical occupations, and for instructional media, presumably so that their instruction would be more efficient.

Still, the 1958 bill did recognize and support secondary-school academic studies that would be ultimately rather than immediately useful. Indeed, the increasing effects of automation on the economy and the concomitant need for retraining displaced workers made some people wonder whether any specific vocational education was appropriate in the secondary school. At the same time, however, the increasing unemployability of young people who dropped out of school created a serious problem by alienating a large number of them from society.

Consequently, although the retention rate or "holding power" of the secondary schools was higher than ever, an increased effort was made to induce these people to remain in, or return to, school. What kind of program the schools should offer them was not clear, but once again it was suggested that the program should be "practical," perhaps involving a combination of work and study. Federal vocational-education legislation in 1963 was the most comprehensive ever enacted. It encompassed all levels from secondary through post-secondary to adult, and embraced many fields, including business, technical subjects, agriculture, home economics, and practical nursing. Not until 1965 did the Congress appropriate funds for general aid to elementary and secondary education, and then primarily for the benefit of schools serving children from low-income families.

Through their elected representatives, and in other ways, the American people reveal their faith in the ability of education to solve specific social problems, their tendency to view education in economic terms, their preference for education that is immediately and unambiguously usable, and their disdain for impractical knowledge that neither puts bread and butter on the table nor solves life's problems. It is true, of course, that the complexity of contemporary life demands more education than did the simpler world of yesterday, and that modern technology requires highly specialized training. So it is hard to convince people that what is most theoretical is often in the long run the most practical, and that the acquisition of complex skills and specialized knowledge demands a long and rigorous program of intellectual development. Indeed, by 1964 one group of scholars had come to the conclusion that the secondary school should eliminate vocational courses and electives altogether and provide all students with a common general education, albeit at different rates and depths.[2]

In the foreseeable future, however, schools will continue to offer many practical subjects, both elective and required. Among them are all subjects taught primarily and explicitly for vocational use, even though they include, or are based on, a body of theory. But in addition schools offer, and will continue to offer, some practical subjects

2 Harry Broudy, B. O. Smith, and Joe Burnett, *Democracy and Excellence in American Secondary Education*, Rand McNally, 1964, p. 36.

for purposes of general education. These include health and physical education, industrial arts and homemaking, and certain aspects of business and agriculture. These courses are practical in the sense that they are primarily concerned with teaching students to carry out specific life activities more effectively. Secondarily, of course, they also teach or reinforce concepts of wider significance.

## PHYSICAL AND HEALTH EDUCATION

The most widely required nonacademic subject is physical education, which has been common in secondary schools since the First World War. Concern about the adequacy of physical-education instruction recurs periodically as selective service rejections are publicized, comparisons are made with European children, and presidential commissions on physical fitness are appointed. It is not always clear to what extent physical education is intended to maintain and improve the present physical fitness of students and to what extent it is intended to teach them how to do so in the future. The latter is clearly an educational aim; the former is not. Nevertheless, the school has a responsibility to see that the health of young people does not deteriorate as a result of the time they spend there. Educators know, too, that good health promotes effective learning.

Most recommendations on physical fitness call for brief daily exercise sessions. Physical-education classes, however, are usually scheduled for longer, less frequent periods. There is some question, therefore, whether both the teaching of skills and knowledge and the maintenance of fitness can be accomplished simultaneously. In fact, secondary schools have been known to schedule students for physical education for one semester and not the other. This practice hardly promotes physical fitness.

Through the increased use of standardized tests, physical-education instructors are able to give attention to the specific activities particular students need most. One simple test measures agility, strength, speed, and endurance. These are aspects of physical fitness that can be improved by appropriate exercises. Many specific physical skills require instruction as well as practice, however. It is possible to teach a person the proper way to dribble and shoot a basketball, to throw and catch a baseball or a football, to serve a tennis ball and drive a golf ball, to aim an arrow, swim the backstroke, and dance a quadrille. Students who are especially well coordinated or have had exceptional opportunities to practice these skills acquire them independently. When physical-education classes are mainly occasions for applying existing skills rather than developing new ones, these students dominate the activities, the less proficient ones are embarrassed, and neither group learns anything. Testing, diagnosis, and individualization of instruction are as important in physical education as in academic subjects.

In the past, overemphasis on team sports led to the neglect both of body-building activities and of recreational skills likely to be of value in adulthood. The emphasis is changing in many places, but there are limits to what can be done where such facilities as swimming pools and tennis courts are not available. Nevertheless, secondary schools generally possess magnificent gymnasiums and playing fields, even though most students are more likely to use them as spectators than as participants.

Although health is taught throughout the elementary-school years, many educators recommend intensive, systematic instruction in health when students are becoming increasingly independent of adults and are consequently being exposed to new hazards and are assuming responsibility for more decisions affecting their health and safety. But whether this instruction should be a classroom adjunct of physical education, whether it should be part of the science program, or whether health should be considered as an academic subject in its own right is a matter of controversy.

At the secondary-school level, health teaching must certainly be something other than indoctrination in superficial rules. Students should learn the basic facts and principles underlying recommended personal and community health practices. That this content be taught by a qualified teacher is more important than the particular format in which the instruction is given. Specialists in health education favor a separate course. With careful planning, however, a secondary school can develop significant understandings pertaining to health in academic courses. Many science teachers are understandably reluctant to incorporate the purely practical aspect of health into their courses. But the fundamentals of human anatomy and physiology, germ theory, and nutrition are important components of most biological science courses. The principles of mental health are probably most appropriately taught by a qualified psychologist. Although psychology is not widely taught in secondary schools, it could easily be defended as an important part of the general education of all people.

Public-health instruction in safety is most effectively given in situations where safety is a concern. It cannot be ignored in shops, laboratories, gymnasiums, kitchens, swimming pools, playgrounds, or any other place where danger is present or hazards exist. On the other hand, driver education, if taught at all, must constitute a separate course. The very effectiveness with which it has been taught gives rise to powerful social and economic arguments for making such a course available to all young people, or even requiring it of them. The arguments are equally strong, however, for having it offered by some agency other than the secondary school.

### PRACTICAL ARTS

Many secondary schools include, among their general education offerings, four practical arts that are closely related to vocational programs: industrial arts, agriculture and horticulture, home economics, and business. Several of these subjects are frequently required of all junior-high-school students, and a comprehensive senior high school may make them all available as electives. Students can also take a major sequence of three or four courses in one of the practical arts instead of in an academic subject.

Courses taught for purposes of general education emphasize the significance of the practical arts in society. Industrial arts classes study the products, procedures, and problems of modern industry. Home economics classes examine the values and problems of contemporary family life. Business courses acquaint students with the functions of management and distribution in the economy. Courses in agriculture stress the relation of that field to industry, business, and the family.

Each of the practical arts also requires students to apply concepts and skills learned in academic subjects. Mathematics and language skills are essential in all of them. Concepts from science, economics, and other disciplines are also needed. One of the values claimed for these courses is that students improve skills and enlarge concepts by applying them. Furthermore, some students are apparently more highly motivated to develop these skills and understandings in academic courses when they recognize their usefulness.

Students devote much of their time in practical arts classes, however, to the acquisition of manipulative skills. When the family was a productive economic unit, children learned the skills of the shop, home, and farm informally as they gradually assumed adult responsibilities. Old ways, some ineffective, were perpetuated. Professionally trained teachers can acquaint students with the latest methods and materials developed by researchers in industry and at universities and experiment stations. And yet, since much of this information is available in magazines and extension service bulletins, many families can still train their children at home, and young people who are able to read can even train themselves. Furthermore, the time that schools can afford for required instruction in the practical arts is seldom great enough to develop real proficiency in students. The skills that must have priority in school are those that contribute most to further learning. Most of these are intellectual in emphasis, and among the practical arts perhaps typewriting most closely meets this requirement.

Enrollments in business education exceed those in all the other practical subjects. This field differs from the others in that it is not usually taught through the use of "projects" to the extent that home economics, agriculture, and industrial arts are. The number of different subjects is also greater in business, and many combinations of them can be used as a major sequence. Usually students specialize either in office-related subjects, such as typewriting, shorthand, and bookkeeping, or in distributive education courses, such as retailing, salesmanship, and advertising. With the exception of typewriting, most of these courses center around skills that are more significant for specific vocational application than for general education. The understandings emphasized in the "introduction to business" and business law courses do have general education implications, however.

Homemaking was originally just cooking and sewing; later, it became known as the study of foods and clothing. Now it is viewed as education for home and family living. Courses or units on family relations, home furnishings, child study, family health, and home management have been added to help boys and girls to develop personally and, later, to create happy homes of their own. Some junior high schools require boys to take homemaking, but few boys elect a homemaking course. Nor is it evident that the homes of the girls who take these courses are any happier than those of other girls. Nevertheless, many of the components of homemaking courses contribute to general education: the psychology of child growth and adolescent development and group behavior, the sociology of the family, the economics of household management, the esthetics of interior decoration and fashion design, and the science of nutrition and health.

Whether this kind of content is best acquired in homemaking classes or in the relevant academic subjects is questionable.

Unlike home economics, agriculture is usually taught for vocational purposes. It is seldom required, and few boys who are not planning to be farmers or to enter one of the numerous agricultural business occupations elect the subject. The arguments for understanding the place of agriculture in the modern world are analogous to those for industrial arts with respect to modern industry. From a nonvocational standpoint, knowledge of the tools and processes by which food and fiber are produced seems at least as significant as comparable knowledge relating to printing and the fabrication of wood, metal, ceramics, plastics, and textiles. Similarly, the suburbanite's lawn and garden are as much a justification for a course in horticulture as his do-it-yourself home workshop is for a woodworking course. Yet industrial arts is considered a part of general education, whereas agriculture is considered so only incidentally.

## VOCATIONAL EDUCATION

The vocational versions of industrial arts are trade and industrial education (T and I) and technical education. These fields, along with homemaking, agriculture, and distributive education, have long been eligible for federal funds under one or more of the vocational-education acts. A distinction is seldom made between trade and industrial subjects, although the former may be viewed as crafts such as carpentry, plumbing, printing, machine work, and dressmaking, whereas the latter include various production activities and repair and maintenance services. This type of vocational education includes more than eighty such specializations. They represent both skilled and unskilled occupations and in general involve a lower ratio of cognitive understanding to manipulative skills than do the subjects comprising technical education. Technical subjects are semiprofessional in nature and include such fields as drafting, electronics, instrumentation, air conditioning, and laboratory technology.

The distinction between vocational and general-education courses in these practical subjects does not lie in the ratio of cognitive to manipulative content, but in the specificity of their application, which is to some extent a function of the depth to which they are pursued. A major sequence in a practical subject for vocational education would consist of six to eight units, or twice what is required for general education. Usually, vocational education is restricted to students in grades 11 and 12, or at least to those who are 16 years of age or older. Typically, a half of each day is devoted to regular required academic subjects or to special instruction in English, mathematics, and science related specifically to the vocational program. In some instances cooperative work experience is made part of the program. Many large cities have separate vocational high schools, and more and more area vocational schools are being established to serve smaller population centers and surrounding rural areas. Nevertheless, the comprehensive high school, which offers both general and vocational education, continues to be favored. Often, however, such schools emphasize business, homemaking, and agriculture and provide only minimal offerings in the trade and technical fields.

Vocational education is expensive. It requires expensive equipment which requires frequent replacement if it is not to become obsolete. Moreover, since there are so many possible subjects, classes tend to be small, and hence uneconomical, unless the school has an extremely large enrollment. In a comprehensive school the enrollment must be great indeed, because a relatively small proportion of the students would be engaged in vocational education aside from business education.

The theoretical justification for the comprehensive school is of course the belief that the presence of young people from varied backgrounds in a single school is a unifying force in our society. Still, this mingling must end at some point, and it may be questioned whether ending it after junior high school rather than after senior high entails any great risk to the society. The practical justification in many districts is that the population does not warrant more than one secondary school. This difficulty is overcome when a number of districts jointly establish a special school for vocational education. And yet the distances that can be traveled daily impose a limit on the size of such a school and, hence, upon its offerings. In any event, no school can offer training in all possible occupations, and whether in a highly mobile society the choice should be based on local employment needs is a debatable question.

It has been estimated that American secondary schools offer some 500 different subjects, of which perhaps 275 are known by the same title in as many as fifteen states.[3] Similar courses have different titles,

---

3 Kenneth Hovet, "What *Are* the High Schools Teaching?" Chapter 3 in *What Shall the High School Teach?* The Association for Supervision and Curriculum Development, 1956, p. 75.

and the same name is used for different courses, but the variation, in any event, is enormous. What is more, some individual schools offer several hundred courses. This multiplicity of offerings is the tangible result of a policy of attempting both to serve a wide range of societal functions and to meet an incredible variety of individual needs. The practical subjects, whether intended for the potential consumer or the potential producer, obviously contribute greatly to the profusion of courses. Yet, of the 275 most common courses, only about 120, or a little over 40 per cent, are in the practical category.

Indeed, another survey[4] revealed that a sample of American high schools gave credit toward graduation for courses with over a thousand different names offered in the upper four years alone, and of these approximately 370 were in the fields here considered practical. By contrast, some 220 titles were used in the field of social studies alone. In part, this may be an indication of uncertainty and confusion in a particular field; in part, it is a predictable consequence of the inevitable lack of standardization in a system of state and local control. But in part, too, variety in course offerings within academic fields is inevitable if adequate recognition is to be given to the great variation in ability found among students.

Doubtless, much of the variation in course titles (and content) is unnecessary and might well be eliminated. Certainly some of the courses listed on students' transcripts are bizarre and hardly suggest anything that a reasonable person would consider deserving of credit for high-school graduation. But a secondary school which, without offering any vocational education, provides general education to all the young people in a community through a variety of courses tailored to every level of ability must surely be regarded as a "comprehensive" school. Indeed, that appellation is almost merited on the basis of the diverse student activities that American secondary schools provide outside, and in addition to, their formal instructional programs.

*Suggestions for Class Discussion and Further Investigation*

1. The movement to vocationalize American secondary schools was extremely powerful in the period between 1907 and 1915. This was a period of exceedingly high immigration, and some have attributed the movement to the strong humanitarian im-

---

[4] Edith Greer and Richard Harbeck, *What High School Students Study*, Bulletin 10, U.S. Office of Education, 1962.

pulses prevalent at that time. It has also been suggested that the vocational emphasis stemmed from an anti-immigrant sentiment among those who controlled the schools. Why might a group that wanted to prevent the rise of the members of lower socio-economic strata promote vocational programs? Is it mere coincidence that the junior-high-school movement began in the same period?

2. Examine a course of study in home economics, agriculture, or industrial arts and see how many of the concepts or skills can be classified under such subject headings as physics, chemistry, biology, economics, psychology, sociology, and mathematics.

3. Suggest how the essential content of home economics, industrial arts, agriculture, and general business could be made a part of a "developmental studies" course dealing with the development of social institutions and modern technology, as proposed by Broudy, Smith, and Burnett (see Suggestions for Further Reading at the end of Chapter One).

### Suggestions for Further Reading

As in the case of academic subjects, each of the subjects considered in this chapter has a literature of its own in methods books and in the journals and yearbooks of professional societies.

Recent federal legislation, coupled with widespread perplexity regarding the kind of vocational preparation that is possible in a rapidly automating technology, has prompted a number of journals to devote entire issues to vocational education. Since the field is in a state of uncertainty and change, the articles in these periodicals may be the best available source of information on the topic: "The New Look in Vocational Education," *Theory into Practice,* 3 (December, 1964), published by The Ohio State University; "The Swing to Vocational-Technical Education," *Phi Delta Kappan,* 46 (April, 1965); and "Vocational Education: Time for Decision," *Bulletin of the National Association of Secondary-School Principals,* 49 (May, 1965). An earlier issue of the *NASSP Bulletin,* 48 (December, 1964), was devoted to "A New Look in Home Economics." The sixty-fourth yearbook of the National Society for the Study of Education, *Vocational Education* (University of Chicago Press, 1965) provides another full treatment.

## Chapter Six

# Student Activities

If anyone tried to learn about American secondary schools by examining a recent high-school yearbook, he would probably conclude that classroom instruction, if there was any, took up very little time and commanded very little attention. The yearbook might have a picture of the school's National Honor Society chapter. But that would probably be the only hint that high-school life did not consist exclusively of athletic contests, student councils, marching bands, debating societies, dramatic productions, senior balls, junior proms, school newspapers, a wide array of clubs, and even, perhaps, sororities and fraternities. The influence of American colleges on the high schools is far more apparent in student life than it is in the program of studies itself.

Most of these student activities seem to have originated with the students themselves. The schools at first discouraged them, but later permitted, and then began to help, students to form groups built around special interests. Before music instruction was common in the schools, many a teacher with an amateur interest in music served as band leader for a group of enthusiastic young musicians. English teachers have traditionally produced and directed student theatricals, coached debating teams, and advised literary societies. Many male teachers have nursed a secret desire to coach an athletic team, and indeed many have supplemented their meager incomes by doing so. Even in the most academically oriented high school there has always been a place for out-of-class activities in which students could develop interests, skills, and qualities of character and leadership. But such schools view student activities with a fine sense of proportion.

Where this sense is lacking, activities tend to get out of hand—"the tail wags the dog." And critics who start by scoring excesses often go on to attack the whole idea of student activities. The pattern is familiar: a good thing is expanded until it becomes too much of a good thing, and as a result the whole is branded a bad thing.

When wise heads prevail, the critical reaction serves as a warning, perspective is restored, and a sensible balance is attained. But in a vast number of American communities, influential elements bent on preserving a source of entertainment or on enhancing their own egos prevent wise heads from prevailing. A school can easily eliminate a French club or curtail intramural sports, but varsity athletic teams and marching bands have powerful supporters. Only a school administrator who is prepared to risk his job can withstand the pressures of alumni and other townsmen with a fierce though distorted sense of local pride, especially when they are abetted by news media and organizations of coaches and musical directors. Student opinion would also be against him, and he would have to contend with the influence of parents whose own feelings of success come chiefly through the success of their children. Indeed, many administrators hold similar values and have no desire to counter these influences, even if they could.

RATIONALE

An administrator may, in fact, be able to rationalize his strong support of extra-class activities by citing the strong emphasis on interests, lifelikeness, and democracy that has dominated the literature on secondary education for many years. Based originally on the principle that interest and effort need not be antithetical in learning, the notion evolved that interest was essential for learning and that classroom activities and even curriculum content should be selected on the basis of students' interests. If "meeting the needs and interests of adolescents" was to be a goal, then clearly an extensive program of extra-class activities was also in order, since these activities give the freest rein to the interests of students.

Furthermore, whereas formal instruction does not lend itself readily to the achievement of such objectives as "worthy use of leisure time," "citizenship," "ethical character," and "health," it seemed likely that clubs, sports, and other activities, involving as they do the pursuit of hobbies, the assumption of responsibility, the exercise of sportsmanship and a cooperative spirit, and, frequently, physical recreation, might serve these ends very well indeed. Moreover, these activities promised an opportunity for students to apply what they learned in class in more nearly "lifelike" situations. If a school sets as a goal the application of learnings in "persistent life situations," certainly the school must give students practice in making applications.

Related to this emphasis on student interests is an exaggerated and seemingly irrelevant concern about democracy. Through student activities the school can teach not merely *about* democracy but democracy itself. The hope is that students who conduct their own organizations and manage the affairs of the student body as a whole will develop "democratic" attitudes and the skills of self-determination. But the emphasis on democracy does not stop there. It is not enough for some educators that schools are free to all and that those who attend are treated equally. They insist that the school as an institution must itself be "democratic," and that it cannot be so unless students are equal partners with adults in determining what is learned and done in the school.

According to this viewpoint, any school that forbids activities in which students wish to engage is "undemocratic"—provided, of course, the activities are not harmful. Furthermore, in order to be truly democratic a school must offer something for everyone, and for students who are not interested in formal instruction extra-class activities are the only reason for remaining in school. Whether this contention is borne out or refuted by data showing that dropouts in general have a poor record of participation in student activities depends on one's interpretation. It can be argued that students who do participate in extra-class activities stay in school for that reason. But it can also be argued that the students who participate in extra-class activities are those who would stay in school anyhow, and hence that such activities do little to retain potential dropouts.

The emphasis on interest, "lifelike" learning situations, and "democracy" led eventually, and paradoxically, to a proposal to eliminate separate student activities. Certain proponents of the core curriculum suggested that there would be no need for an extra-class program if classes were conducted in an informal, club-like atmosphere in which students helped plan learning activities that were in line with their interests. But few schools have eliminated activities because of the increasing informality of classes. More often, activities have changed status by becoming more formal. Some activities, such as musical performance groups, journalism clubs, and photography clubs are often conducted like noncredit courses, and many schools have made them a regular part of the program of studies.

Although the distinction between class and extra-class activities is not always sharp, these activities differ in several important ways. Participation in student activities is optional; enrollment in classes is not. Performance in courses is evaluated by means of grades, and grades have a bearing on promotion and graduation; this is not true of performance in student activities. Classroom instruction must be professionally planned and directed; activities can be planned and carried out by the students themselves with the advice, guidance, and assistance of teacher-sponsors. When clubs become too class-like they lose much of their potential value. So do classes when they become too club-like.

CHARACTERISTICS

The basic aims of classroom instruction are different from those of extra-class activities. To be sure, certain activities supplement and reinforce class instruction and thus contribute in a minor way to intellectual development. But this is not the chief reason for promoting student activities. If their aims were primarily intellectual, it might be more sensible for schools to add instructional time than to maintain an activities program. An instructional class consists of individual learners, whereas students participating in extra-class activities constitute an action group. Although each member of a class pursues learning goals of his own, the class as a group has no goal. Action groups, on the other hand, have purposes that are achieved either in or through their activities. Usually, the learning that occurs is implicit in the situation.

At a school dance or in a dramatics club, for example, adolescents learn social skills and develop social attitudes that are expected of them in our American culture. Though most students want to acquire these skills and attitudes, the goal of the school dance is the dance itself, not the learnings it provides, and with the dramatics club "the play's the thing." By contrast, classroom activities are essential to the attainment of explicit learning outcomes.

Many extra-class activities give students a chance to formulate plans and carry them out. Learning to assume responsibility is implicit in such activities. Since a sense of responsibility is an essential attribute of both an educated man and a democratic citizen, and since the only way to inculcate it is to give students frequent opportunities to exercise responsibility, secondary schools should provide an abundance of such experiences. These are the years *par excellence* for pressing this objective, for it is during this time that students are becoming acutely aware of their identity as individuals and increasingly desirous of freeing themselves from adult domination and control. Children who have been overly dependent on their parents find it difficult to become responsible individuals. Unless they are helped to do so during the high-school years they may remain irresponsible.

Letting students assume responsibility often conflicts with the desires of adults for efficiency of procedures and excellence of performance. The temptation is nearly irresistible for teachers to intervene in order to expedite an enterprise or assure a polished product. Understandably, adults wish to spare young people from committing errors, and yet it is only when mistakes are permitted that young people learn responsible behavior. A complex, technological society deprives its young of a responsible role; schools must not do likewise.

Thus, again, the specific nature and ostensible purpose of particular activities are educationally less important than the conditions under which they are pursued. When a school seeks to achieve specific learning outcomes through extra-class activities, adults must assume the major responsibility for planning and directing those activities. But by so doing they rob the activities of their chief value. The primary reason for publishing a school newspaper is not to train students in journalism or to interest them in a journalistic career. Such goals might be achieved more systematically and thoroughly through an elective course. The primary justification for the existence of the newspaper is that it offers students an opportunity to engage in an enterprise which demands careful planning, coordinated scheduling, allocation of tasks, and acceptance of individual responsibility. The enterprise, if successful, may result in a better school spirit, improved public relations, and interscholastic recognition. But these effects are secondary. The success of the activity, which could be assured by the constant intervention of teachers, is of far less significance than the students' effort to make it a success. This principle applies to such other activities as athletics, student government, assemblies, dramatics, and the meetings of the humblest club. An activity sponsor should do as little as possible so that students may do (and learn) as much as possible.

In applying this principle, one must of course make due allowance for the maturity of the pupils. Beginning seventh-graders who have had little experience in managing their own activities need help in learning how to do so. How much help is still required by senior-high-school students is a fair indication of the success of the junior-high-school activities program. Because younger pupils need to learn the basic skills of participation and leadership, and because their interests differ from those of older students, six-year secondary schools find it desirable to carry on one program of activities for the junior high school and another program for the senior high school.

Many schools entrust the overall direction of student activities to the student leadership group. Sometimes a student council, with the approval of the principal, prescribes formal procedures for "chartering" clubs and other activities. The students themselves formulate rules governing participation, office-holding, fund-raising, and the like. Seldom are students permitted to schedule the activities, although it might be good experience for senior-high-school students to have to satisfy conflicting demands and to adjudicate disagreements. Some schools have developed elaborate point systems for the dual purpose of controlling participation and recognizing leadership. These schemes involve so much administrative and clerical attention, however, that they are difficult to justify unless they are completely in the hands of the students themselves. If high-school students are not able to accept such responsibility, the student activities program has failed to achieve one of its main purposes.

It is incongruous that schools so often find it necessary to use rigid controls and extrinsic incentives in a program that is supposed to promote responsibility through activities of inherent interest to students. True, no program can fully realize this ideal. But we may well ask whether we can even approach the ideal by following practices that are contrary to it. Students whose values and judgments are so immature that they flagrantly overparticipate need individual counseling more than they need arbitrary rules. They must learn to manage their time, husband their energies, and put first things first, without the aid of regulations.

Similarly, they must learn to participate in an activity because of the values that are inherent in the participation itself rather than for any extraneous recognition or rewards. The rewards for service lie in the serving. Good citizenship is a duty for which no prizes are to be expected. Recreation has no ends outside itself, however beneficial it may be to physical fitness and mental health. These lessons assume special significance in a nation of joiners, most of whom are inactive members of innumerable organizations held together by small, faithful minorities trying desperately to stimulate interest and enlarge membership. It is not necessary that all student activities take place in groups or that all groups be highly organized. The school has many facilities that students would like to use more often —if they had the time. The activities program might well enable individuals and unorganized groups to pursue interests in laboratories, libraries, shops, and art studios to their hearts' content.

When a high-school activities program fails to arouse the enthusiasm of students, several questions need to be asked. Is the program needed at all? In communities where the majority of the young people are caught up in so many organized activities outside school that they have little time to themselves, there may be little or no justification for an activities program in the school. There the need is for a limited program to serve those students who for one reason or another are left out of community activities. In communities that offer young people few opportunities for constructive group activities, however, a more extensive school program may be needed.

A second question: Is the program appropriate? In general, student interest is the chief determinant of which activities are suitable. Well-established activities tend to persist from year to year, but changing conditions sometimes make it wise to eliminate certain activities, introduce new ones, and resume some that had previously been discontinued. Many schools survey students' interests annually and try at least to satisfy each student's second choice if not his first. Teachers with special interests of their own often stimulate students to explore areas they themselves would not have suggested. Enthusiastic students also stimulate others to join them by means of personal persuasion or through exhibits and assembly presentations. Counselors can deal with the occasional shy, uninformed, or lethargic pupil who fails to participate, but widespread apathy should prompt a review of the entire program. The faculty must determine whether its scope and composition are appropriate, whether it is properly conducted, and, indeed, whether it is needed at all.

## STUDENT GOVERNMENT

It is common in American secondary schools to permit students to share in the government of the school community. Although democratic motives usually prompt such an arrangement, pupils clearly have no *right* to govern themselves, nor is the ultimate *responsibility* of school officials diminished by granting them a voice in government. Giving students some responsibility for the direction of various facets of school life mitigates certain problems of school management and control and fosters such desirable qualities of citizens as self-reliance, leadership, cooperation, initiative, and responsibility.

Ordinarily, student government centers around a student council consisting of officers elected on a school-wide basis and of members who represent such constituencies as grades, homerooms, and social-studies classes. All students of the school are usually considered to be "citizens," although in some schools membership in the General Organization (G.O.) or Student Association is contingent on the payment of a tax or fee, in return for which students may receive certain admission tickets, publications, or other privileges without charge or at a reduced cost. Most frequently, though, the purchase of an activities card or ticket is optional and is unrelated to citizenship status.

The problem of financing student activities in a public school is a vexing one. Students who pay a tax experience one of the realities of political life and may appreciate activities more because they have a greater stake in them. Usually, however, neither value is realized, because the students merely obtain the money from their parents and make no sacrifice themselves. Also, whenever there is a general assessment, or whenever dues, participation fees, or admission charges are levied for individual activities and events, some students are unable or disinclined to participate; thus a situation is created that is inconsistent with the principles of democracy and free public education. The expenses incident to attendance in public high schools, sometimes referred to as "hidden tuition costs," are greater than is generally realized, and they probably contribute to the decision of some students to drop out of school.

Many secondary schools prefer to have students engage in money-making projects to support their activities. All too often, however, earning money becomes the chief concern of student groups, to the detriment of their true purposes. Nor is it easy to find profitable schemes that do not result in annoying, and often unreasonable, demands upon local merchants, parents, and neighbors. All in all, a strong case can be made for supporting student activities through the regular school budget. But, whatever the source of the money, it is a valuable experience for student leaders to decide how the funds should be apportioned.

### ATHLETICS

It is extremely difficult to be objective about high-school or college athletics. There seems to be no neutral position between that of the detractors, to whom athletics are completely irrelevant to education and a shameful waste of students' time and school funds, and the supporters, to whom commencement is a sad occasion marked by the loss of valuable lettermen. The supporters make numerous claims for athletics. In addition to their presumed contribution to physical fitness, athletics are said to provide adolescents with a release for excess emotional energy; to develop sportsmanship, teamwork, the "will to win," a competitive spirit, and sundry other character traits;

to entice potential drop-outs to stay in school; to stimulate "school spirit"; and to prepare for lifelong enjoyment as a participant or as a spectator. The detractors counter by charging that only a small minority of students have an opportunity to participate in sports, that girls are neglected almost entirely, that the pressure to win creates emotional tensions or at least perverts the ideals of sportsmanship, that playing games is not a sufficient reason for remaining in school, that the glorification of athletic prowess promotes a false sense of values, and that the sports emphasized in school are not those that most people play or watch as adults.

These criticisms are leveled almost exclusively at abuses in interscholastic athletics. Seldom does anyone deny the value of sports in the lives of either adolescents or adults. When education-oriented coaches are safeguarded from unenlightened community pressures, they join their faculty colleagues in promoting a broad and vigorous intramural program as an extension of a varied program of physical education and as a base for a defensible interscholastic athletics program. All three programs should be directed by a professional physical-education staff, although the assistance of other teachers is usually needed. The active participation of faculty members enhances the value of the whole program and helps keep athletic activities in proper perspective.

State and league organizations usually regulate interscholastic athletics in an effort to protect the health and safety of participants and to assure fair competition. Even so, teachers have reason to be concerned when students lose sleep, neglect homework, or miss classes in order to play in games scheduled during school hours or on school nights. Perhaps the greatest imposition on teachers, however, is requiring them to judge individually the eligibility of students. In enforcing eligibility rules the faculty should, in fairness to individual teachers, act as a whole or by committee; and in fairness to coaches and players, the faculty should act well before the day of a game.

That there should be criteria for eligibility is seldom questioned. Students who do not live up to their responsibilities as citizens of the school should not represent it on athletic teams or in any other way. Similarly, those who neglect their studies should be denied the privilege of participating in varsity sports, both in their own interest and to keep values straight in the school. Whether this means insisting that athletes maintain a specified average depends on the school's marking system. Students who are doing the best they can academically should not be penalized for failing to attain a mark that is unattainable. Furthermore, the meaning of a given average differs from school to school in the same league and from student to student in the same school, depending on the student's program.

So long as colleges continue to maintain extensive programs of athletic competition, the elimination of varsity sports at the senior-high-school level cannot reasonably be expected. The best that concerned teachers can do is to try to control them, to understand why they appeal to students, and to help students understand that other values have precedence in the school. At the junior-high-school level there is a strong sentiment against extensive and highly organized interscholastic sports programs. Medical authorities object to any vigorous contact sports during this period of rapid growth, when heart and bones are susceptible to injury. Some psychologists object to the emotional pressures of public competitive events. The "play day" format, which is used for girls' sports in both junior and senior high schools, might be appropriate for junior-high-school boys. Under this arrangement, students who excel in a sport are given an opportunity to meet and play with, as well as against, students of comparable skill from other schools. Many junior high schools schedule informal interscholastic games which are played before student spectators only during school hours. Still, imitative varsity programs are multiplying at this level. Unfortunately, they are often under the control of high-school athletic directors instead of junior-high-school principals.

An interscholastic program can serve as an outlet for athletic excellence, in the same way that honors courses do for academic excellence. The intramural program provides both a training ground for students with athletic talent and an opportunity for the less talented to participate for the fun of it. The inclusion of such sports as tennis, archery, gymnastics, skating, softball, ping-pong, bowling, and swimming provides for individual competition, participation by boys and girls together, and the development of skills that will be useful in later life. Tournaments, leagues with carefully matched teams, and simple informal play all have a place in such a program. Playoffs between leading teams and contests between students and energetic faculty members heighten interest in the program throughout the school. Competition and interest are usually greater when teams represent homerooms, to which students attach their loyalties. Since it is often difficult to arrange equal-sized and evenly matched teams from homerooms, some schools devise a system whereby points for individual participation and winning are credited to homerooms.

## HOMEROOMS AND ASSEMBLIES

Although membership is not voluntary, the homeroom serves as a setting for student activities that are not a part of the formal instructional program. Many schools use the homeroom merely as an administrative device for taking attendance, making announcements, and taking care of other routines, and a fair number use it as the basic constituency for student government. But most teachers do not know what else to do in a homeroom, and few administrators give them any direction or assistance. Consequently, homeroom programs are often ineffective, and most schools do not attempt them at all. Still, there are sound arguments for the homeroom.

Because secondary schools are departmentalized, teachers seldom concern themselves with how a student performs in the over-all school situation. Moreover, because secondary schools tend to form class sections according to students' abilities, class groups seldom reflect the heterogeneity of society or indeed of the school itself. Each guidance specialist commonly serves from 300 to 500 students, which means that he cannot possibly provide either counseling or information to all students on an individual basis. For all these reasons, the homeroom—with a heterogeneous student population, with a teacher concerned about the members as individuals, and with time set aside for providing information, discussing problems, and counseling students informally—could be made to serve a worthwhile purpose.

At the junior-high-school level the homeroom helps to reduce the abruptness of change from the elementary school. Shifting for the first time from teacher to teacher, and often to a different group for each class, the younger students need to have some group to which they feel they belong and some teacher they feel knows them well. In the senior high school the homeroom is undoubtedly less important, yet it might well be continued, since students can virtually run it themselves and it can still serve worthwhile purposes. Studies have shown, for example, that many students drop out of school without anyone's being aware of their intention to do so. Dropouts often express the belief that no one in the school cared one way or the other whether they left. Students would be less likely to leave unexpectedly or to feel unwanted if their homeroom teachers made a point of getting to know them personally, of referring to a guidance specialist

those who need help, and of encouraging the members of the homeroom group to discuss common problems and to show concern for
fellow members.

Nevertheless, teachers hesitate to initiate or encourage discussions
of topics that are not directly related to their own subjects. Some
feel insecure in any group discussion that does not follow formal
parliamentary procedures. Others feel that they lack the information
they need to protect students from reaching invalid conclusions. Still
others feel unsure about what topics are of concern to students.
Teachers should not be blamed for these feelings of inadequacy,
nor should homeroom programs be abandoned because of them.
Competent administrators and counselors can train teachers to detect student concerns and can furnish information about common
problems; and teachers themselves can acquire, through practice,
skill in conducting group discussions, especially if they are given
some guidance in sound procedures. Since such discussions provide
an ideal opportunity to give guidance in a group setting, the help
teachers need to take advantage of the opportunity should come
from the school's guidance specialists. On them must fall the responsibility for the effectiveness of the homeroom program—unless, of
course, the teachers are so lacking in interest that they are unwilling
to cooperate.

Teachers who question the value of a homeroom program might
ask themselves whether any other scheme offers a better opportunity
to introduce a personal, human touch into a mass educational process that is inevitably impersonal. Some people would have every subject class deal with students' personal problems and all aspects of
development. Others would combine subjects and incorporate guidance into the resulting block of time. Both these approaches detract
from the systematic study of a subject. In order that intellectual
development may have priority in the instructional program, schools
must meet the other expectations held of them through such means
as extra-class activities, guidance services, and homerooms.

Nevertheless, not all teachers should be expected to take charge
of a homeroom. Some who are excellent teachers of their subject are
not effective counselors or group leaders. These teachers should assume additional instructional responsibility or perform other duties
so that those who are better suited might take responsibility for two
homeroom groups, if necessary. Actually, many teachers who feel
inadequate could manage a homeroom if they had a clear idea of
what they were supposed to do and were helped to learn how to do

it. Merely by accepting responsibility for knowing the progress and problems of one group of students, a teacher can make the homeroom a communications link with the home and a coordinating center for activities, guidance, and the instructional programs.

Just as the homeroom can coordinate the school program for the individual student, the assembly can coordinate it for the student body as a whole. A vestige of the daily chapel exercises of earlier days, the assembly is now seldom scheduled more frequently than once every two weeks. It is perhaps best used for ceremonial occasions and for convocations related to student government, and for student presentations that are worthy of a wide audience. Occasionally, guest speakers and professional performances are appropriate, especially in rural areas where cultural opportunities are not readily available. Such programs should not be too frequent, however, and students should not be charged admission.

Far more suitable than commercial programs are presentations by classes and by student groups with special interests and talents. For example, musical programs, dramatic productions, debates, science demonstrations, historical skits, and gymnastic exhibitions afford large numbers of students an opportunity to learn how to conduct themselves before an audience. At the same time, those in the audience learn courteous and appreciative behavior, as well as whatever the presentation teaches them. Assembly programs should be enjoyable, but they should be regarded as educational experiences rather than as entertainment. They are of most value when they are planned, conducted, and presented by students, with a minimum of guidance from teachers.

## Suggestions for Class Discussion and Further Investigation

1. Review your own experience with student government at the secondary and collegiate levels, whether as a leader, active participant, apathetic observer, or scoffing critic. Does participation in student government have any educational value? Under what circumstances? What would constitute evidence of whether or not it is "successful"?

2. Should all secondary-school teachers be expected to sponsor a club or serve as adviser to some student activity? If so, what should be done with respect to those who refuse? If not, how should the student-activities program be conducted? Or should such activities be abolished?

3. Select an activity you would be interested in leading. Outline

what you would hope to accomplish, what your role would be in relation to that of the students, and what kinds of activity the group would engage in.

4. Examine your attitude toward interscholastic athletic competition. Should it be abolished? If so, why? What effect do you think its abolition would have? If you feel that it should be retained, on what basis do you advocate its retention? What limitations or safeguards would you insist upon?

5. What opportunities for professional service do you see in the homeroom situation that you do not see in the subject classroom? What educational use you would make of a daily five-minute interval with a homeroom group? Of a weekly forty-minute period?

6. Is the development of school loyalty a desirable goal? If not, why not? If so, can assemblies be effective in promoting this aim? Is this their chief justification? If not, what is? Through what other means can loyalty be promoted?

7. Obtain a list of the student activities that exist in a specific secondary school. Classify the activities on some basis and judge the adequacy of the program with respect to the total number and the balance of opportunities available. Which specific activities would you consider of questionable value?

## Suggestions for Further Reading

One of the more informative books on student activities is *The Third Curriculum: Student Activities in American Education,* by Robert W. Frederick (Appleton-Century-Crofts, 1959). A recent issue of the *Bulletin of the National Association of Secondary-School Principals,* 48 (October, 1964) was devoted to "Student Activities in Today's Schools." The opening chapter, by Grace Graham, "Student Activities—An Overview and a Rationale" (pp. 1–16), examines the place of such activities in modern education.

The principals' organization publishes a handbook on student council activities, *The Student Council in the Secondary School* (NASSP, 1962). A handbook for advisers of activities has been prepared by Everett M. Shepherd, *How To Sponsor Student Activities* (Henington Publishing Company, 1960).

## Chapter Seven

# Student Personnel Services

It is all too easy, in discussions of educational objectives, school organization, and curricular practices, to lose sight of the students. In the school itself students can hardly be ignored as a group, but the individual student may easily be overlooked. The program of extra-class activities stresses students' interests and gives them a chance to assume responsibility, but, again, most of these activities are group-oriented. With the exception of the effective homeroom, none of them centers attention explicitly on the student as a human being.

Yet the absence notation in the attendance register represents a real person who is absent for some reason, and behind each test score in the list that can be so readily averaged is a real person. It is a human being who makes errors because he can't see the blackboard, who is afraid of his algebra teacher, who is planning to leave school on his sixteenth birthday, who has no friends in school, who falls asleep in class, and who must choose which one of some two thousand colleges he should attend or which of the thirty thousand occupations he should consider as his life work. One student has a room of his own; another doesn't have a bed of his own. This one is repeating French I and failing geometry, but his college-educated parents insist that he attend a well-known college; that one is an honor student, but his parents see no value in college. One girl cries because a B in music spoiled her straight-A record; another seems unconcerned that her average has inexplicably dropped from B to D in the past year. Each individual's situation is unique.

Some of the problems that students experience originate in the school itself. Others stem from factors unrelated to the school, and yet they affect a student's performance in school. Schools can prevent some problems from arising, can help students cope with others, and can cooperate with other agencies in alleviating still others. But even where nothing whatsoever can be done, merely for school per-

sonnel to know that a given student has a problem can be helpful
to him.

## ORGANIZED SERVICES

In order to help individual students deal with personal problems
and to plan intelligently, most secondary schools now provide a
variety of student personnel services. Specialized personnel assist and
supplement the teaching staff. Increasingly, these specialists work as
a team in an organized personnel services unit. The principal members are the school nurse and doctor, the attendance officer, the
guidance counselor, and the school psychologist. Other members may
include a school social worker or visiting teacher, remedial reading
and speech teachers, and a dental hygienist.

This service unit may have a designated director. Even so, it is
usually the guidance specialists who coordinate the various services.
Students in need of help tend to come first to the guidance personnel, who often consult with the other specialists or refer students to
them. Whatever his particular technical specialty, each of the pupil
personnel specialists also serves a guidance function. Teachers, too,
engage in guidance activities.

The attitudes of teachers toward guidance and related services
reflect their views regarding the objectives of the school. Those who
would limit the school's purpose to intellectual development reject
all services except those that are needed to enforce the law and to
protect students while they are in school. They feel that the school
fulfills its obligations if it offers educational opportunities, and that
taking advantage of them is up to the student and his parents.

At the other extreme are those who hold the school broadly responsible for meeting all the needs of all the students. They consider
health, happiness, vocational success, social adjustment, and emotional stability to be legitimate objectives of the school. To them,
guidance and education are almost synonymous.

Most teachers probably adopt a position somewhere between
these extremes. They do not consider the school a welfare agency,
but they do hold it responsible both for providing educational opportunities and for helping students to take maximum advantage of
them. The school must make every effort to assure that no student is
deprived of the full benefit of a secondary education by unwise decisions or remediable conditions. On a matter as important as educa-

tion, young people should not suffer because of the negligence or ignorance of adults at home or in school.

Making student personnel services instrumental rather than ends in themselves does not mean that finding solutions for students' specific, immediate problems is their only concern. No one wishes to prolong or increase the students' dependence on adults. Associated with the service function is the instructional task of teaching students how to solve their own problems independently. School nurses are usually required to have special preparation in education as well as in nursing, and most guidance counselors have had classroom teaching experience. It is essential that teachers and specialists understand each other's purposes and problems and work together closely for the students' benefit.

## GUIDANCE BY TEACHERS

Good teachers are always concerned about their students as individuals. Students seek their counsel and often receive unsolicited advice from them, though much of that advice is undoubtedly poor. The world grows more complex with every year, and to say what one would do "if I were you" requires either great wisdom or great courage. This does not mean that teachers should not provide guidance. They do, however, need some training for this role, and even then they need the assistance of specialists. Just because a school employs guidance specialists is no reason for teachers to assume that they themselves have no responsibility for guiding students.

There are certain guidance functions which specialists can perform far better than teachers can. There are others which teachers can perform better, and still others on which specialists and teachers must cooperate. In addition to helping students directly, specialists help teachers do a better job of both guidance and instruction. In turn, they depend on teachers for help. But in the long run specialists exist for the benefit of teachers rather than the other way around.

For example, what kind of services can the secondary-school teacher expect from specialists? For one thing, he can expect them to be able to give him information about students. By checking with the guidance office, a teacher who is particularly concerned about a student should be able to obtain information that is routinely recorded and should also be able to find out what other teachers or the counselors have learned about the student in their dealings with him. The counselors are able to help the teacher interpret test data and other information. They may be able to suggest possible explanations for a student's behavior and to predict the probable consequences of various courses of action that the teacher might take with respect to a student. If the teacher needs more than information and advice, a specialist may be able to help by counseling the student.

A good counselor is interested in the progress and behavior of students and is pleased when a teacher takes a special interest in one of them. He wants teachers to consult him when he can be of help, especially when they realize that they lack the necessary competence to deal with a given problem. He does not want them merely to turn problems over to him as if they had no responsibility for trying to help students. On the other hand, he wants to be advised about a situation before it gets out of hand. But above all a counselor wants teachers to be realistic about what he can and cannot do. Some problems simply cannot be solved, and with many the progress is slow and the results only partially satisfactory. The counselor is no magician. Furthermore, he usually needs a great deal of help from teachers.

One way in which a teacher can help guidance specialists is by being alert to signs of difficulty on the part of his students. Teachers are the first to note when students encounter academic difficulties. Inexplicable declines in achievement usually warrant investigation. Truancy is almost always serious, and frequent tardiness requires explanation. Alert teachers can often detect health problems, and they can hardly fail to notice behavior that may be symptomatic of emotional difficulties. Whether a student requires treatment or counseling or merely bears watching, guidance specialists depend on teachers to recognize his need for help.

Moreover, specialists rely on teachers to provide much of the information they need in their work with students. They also rely on teachers to transmit information to students bearing on decisions and adjustments they are called on to make. In orienting new students, information about the school and its procedures must be provided and explained. When students plan their high-school programs, information about available offerings and requirements must be made available. At other times students need facts about colleges, scholarships, vocations, and those aspects of their development about which they are particularly concerned. Given timely and reliable information, most students can handle their problems and can make appropriate decisions with little, if any, counseling. Generally pertinent information is most efficiently provided in a group setting like the homeroom, instead of individually.

Formal courses provide students with information relating to their problems. Facts about physical development are presented in health and science courses. Much can be learned about behavior in the study of literature, and both biography and fiction depict various occupations. Some social-studies courses include occupational data in a social or economic context, and in almost every subject teachers often have occasion to point out occupations to which the material being studied is relevant. Since teachers are poorly equipped to inform students accurately about some of the matters on which they need guidance, they must rely on printed materials furnished by guidance specialists. The guidance office can also supply or recommend books and pamphlets which teachers can give to individual students who need a specific kind of information.

Teachers do more, however, than merely aid the guidance specialists. They frequently deal with individual students and groups in a guidance relationship. Opportunities for individual counseling arise when students turn for help to a teacher with whom they have especially good rapport. To be a good counselor the teacher often merely needs to be an interested listener. With a group, he needs primarily to be a skillful leader.

Guidance is not essentially a matter of giving advice, but rather a process of assisting individuals to clarify and accept problems in order that they may deal with them rationally. An individual student may achieve such clarification and acceptance by talking with a teacher about his problem. By discussing a shared problem, members of a group can bring out various facts and suggest a number of possible approaches. Such discussions may provide a student with needed information and show him how problems can be attacked in a rational manner. More important, perhaps, a student learns through such discussion that problems he thought were uniquely his are bothering his classmates also. This awareness does not remove the problems, but it often makes them easier to live with. Clearly, when a teacher believes a student has a problem which no amount of group discussion or counseling by the teacher can solve, he has the responsibility of referring the student to a guidance specialist.

## GUIDANCE BY SPECIALISTS

Teachers are trained to help students to learn, not to help them solve their problems. Although most teachers are interested in their students as individuals and willing to help them in any way they can, willingness is not always enough. Specialized knowledge and skills are often necessary. The so-called "world of work" is complex and ever-changing, and teachers cannot be expected to know the outlook and requirements for the many occupational fields. Getting into college is becoming increasingly complicated and competitive, and most teachers are not familiar with either the admissions policies and procedures of the numerous institutions or the strategy and tactics of making applications. The large comprehensive high school offers students many choices of programs and subjects and also imposes various prerequisites and graduation requirements. Again, teachers would have difficulty keeping abreast of these matters or of so specialized and technical a field as standardized testing. Furthermore, counseling is itself an art which few busy teachers have occasion to master. Because teachers lack the knowledge, skill, and time to provide all the guidance services which high-school students require, most secondary schools have at least one guidance specialist on the staff. Indeed, authorities recommend that there be one for every 250 to 300 students in the school, but on the average the actual ratio is nearer twice these figures.

Organized guidance by specialists is generally considered to have begun in 1908, when Frank Parsons established his "Vocational Bureau" in Boston to help drifting boys find careers. Within a few years schools began to form similar bureaus. The classical guidance paradigm, as formulated by Parsons, had three elements. On the one side was an inventory of the individual's assets and liabilities, on the other was accurate information about vocational opportunities. These two elements were brought together in a counseling interview. Guidance specialists still devote most of their time to this trio of concerns: inventory, information, and interviews.

The core of the *individual inventory* is a cumulative record for each student. The student's folder can contain only the information that is most likely to be of value when a specific problem arises. The counselor can obtain additional data from teachers, parents, and other sources, including the student being counseled. But if some kinds of information were not preserved over a student's entire school career, they would be impossible to obtain when they were needed. Consequently, records must be started in the elementary school and maintained straight through secondary school. They usually contain information on the student's family background, a record of his academic progress and his participation in school activities, health data, descriptive summaries by each of his former teachers, standardized test results, anecdotal accounts of significant incidents in his life, and memoranda on counseling sessions. In addition, they include the student's choice of a high-school program, his tentative vocational decisions, his plans for education beyond high school, and, sometimes, brief autobiographical statements.

The most expensive and time-consuming items to obtain are the results of standardized tests. Testing programs differ from school to school, but most schools use group tests to get at least three estimates of each student's scholastic aptitude beween the fourth and tenth grades. Usually they administer achievement batteries, consisting of anywhere from five to ten separate tests, once a year, or at least once every two years. These batteries include tests in reading and tests in a number of other basic subjects. The chief value of accumulating standardized test results is that they provide a continuing record of each student's development. Unfortunately, many schools simply tabulate the results as noncomparable scores at irregular intervals, thus making it virtually impossible to perceive patterns. A more useful way to record scores is to display them graphically, so that they may be readily compared and so that a student's departure from his normal channel of development reveals itself clearly.

The results of these regularly scheduled tests serve various purposes. Properly interpreted, they help a school to evaluate its over-all effectiveness, to diagnose its instructional needs, and to determine appropriate groupings. In guidance, however, their purpose is to increase self-understanding on the part of students. Counselors administer additional tests individually to students whenever it seems likely that the students can understand and use the information the tests provide about them.

Just as records and tests help the student understand himself, the *information service* is designed to help him become aware of educational and vocational opportunities. Guidance offices make available to students a collection of current college catalogs and an up-to-date occupational file. Supplementing the catalogs are directories listing institutions of higher learning, information on scholarships and financial aids, and publications on how to plan for college. The occupational file consists of monographs, briefs, and abstracts that give information on specific occupations: qualifications, salaries and working conditions, preparation, and other information that students need for vocational planning. This basic file is supplemented by the United States Department of Labor's *Dictionary of Occupational Titles,* books about careers, pamphlets on employment trends, and bibliographies of additional sources of information.

In addition to materials on education and vocations, guidance specialists bring together books and pamphlets on health, manners, personality, mental hygiene, marriage, and social skills. They also arrange for the showing of films on special subjects, organize field trips to industrial plants and college campuses, and invite informed spokesmen to the school for "career day" and "college night" programs.

Although professional guidance workers spend a great deal of time maintaining records, administering tests, and conducting an information service, they regard counseling as their most important function. The individual *counseling interview* (or, occasionally, the group counseling session) is to the counselor what the lesson is to the teacher. He holds in strict confidence all that transpires in his face-to-face interviews with students. His aim is to establish a rapport that will enable him to foster in the counselee enough insight and self-understanding for him to recognize, define, and accept his problems, assess alternatives, formulate tentative decisions and plans, and commit himself to a course of action that can be reviewed and revised in subsequent interviews.

Probably no two counselors have exactly the same notion of what the interview should be. Certainly no two interviews are identical. But the counselor should at least make the counselee aware of what to expect from the interview. Many members of the public—and even some teachers—have an erroneous conception of what the counselor can and cannot do. Some critics question whether anything at all can be accomplished through counseling. More often, however, people expect counselors to "steer" students into the proper "channels" or to "make them" suddenly change their behavior. Counseling, at its best, is not authoritarian. Nor can it work miracles. The counselee must realize this if he is to get any benefit from an interview.

During the 1940's two schools of thought developed regarding counseling. The leading advocates of the opposing viewpoints were two psychologists, E. G. Williamson and Carl Rogers. Intellectually, most guidance counselors lean toward the Rogerian "client-centered" view. In practice, most probably use an eclectic approach.

The client-centered approach is nondirective. It assumes that the counselee has within himself the power to solve his own problems and make his own decisions, and that no one else can, or has the right to, do these things for him. Nondirective counseling aims at helping the counselee gain insight into himself and the situation he faces so that he can release this power. In the interview, the counselor takes great care not to seize the initiative. He echoes the counselee's statements and sometimes merely indicates that he has heard them. Eventually, the client talks his problem through and commits himself to a course of action.

By contrast, the clinical approach to counseling places the counselor in a role analogous to that of a physician. After assembling all the data and diagnosing the problem, he issues a prescription. He gives advice, but only after he has weighed the facts carefully. This is not the offhand counsel of a well-meaning but only partially informed adult. In many instances the recommended decision is undoubtedly sounder than that which the student would make alone, or even with the help of his parents. Certainly the student is better off following the counselor's advice than he is when he merely copies the behavior of his friends. The directive counselor hopes, therefore, that the student will readily concur with his recommendations once the basis for them has been explained. He uses persuasion, if necessary, to convince the student that he should accept them.

Competent guidance specialists try to avoid being overly directive, because they are reluctant to assume responsibility for determining the course of another person's life. Moreover, one of their aims is to help students learn to make their own decisions, and they realize that a counselor-centered approach is more likely to increase dependence than to reduce it. Many secondary schools actually authorize guidance personnel to require that students follow the courses of action they recommend, particularly in the choice of high-school programs. And sometimes counselors have the power to punish students for unacceptable conduct. When students see the counselor in these authoritative roles they are unlikely to accord him the confidence that is essential to the counseling relationship. Not even a

parent can induce his children to turn freely to him for help in time
of trouble if they perceive him chiefly as a punitive figure; and the
professional counselor does not command the affection that is usually present in the parent-child relationship.

On the other hand, the school counselor obviously cannot be entirely nondirective either. Such counseling requires a great deal of
time. Counselors are responsible for large numbers of students, and
they cannot give any one of them a disproportionate amount of their
time. Moreover, many decisions a student is called upon to make,
such as what program to take or what college to attend, must be
made by a specified time. They cannot be put off until the student
gains the necessary insight and maturity to make them himself.
While not making the decision for the student, the counselor may
have to take the lead in getting him to reach one.

In practice, secondary-school counselors usually choose a course
between the extremely nondirective approach and the clinical approach, being guided by the nature of the problem at hand and the
characteristics of the student. In addition to helping the student
solve an immediate problem, the conscientious counselor tries to
promote long-range growth toward mature self-sufficiency; he tries
to deal with the underlying sources of problems as well as with their
manifestations.

The distinction between guidance and counseling is not sharp.
But, strictly speaking, guidance is possible only with students who
are emotionally prepared to deal with problems on a relatively objective and realistic basis. Counseling consists of bringing students
to the point where they can profit from guidance, by increasing their
insight and by helping them to alter their perceptions of themselves
and the world. The guidance specialist provides both guidance and
counseling.

Although teachers usually lack both the time and the competence
to engage in extensive counseling, they can render an important
service by referring troubled students to the guidance specialist. The
specialist, in turn, will refer to the school psychologist any children
whose problems are complex and whose troubles lie deep. If there is
no psychologist on the school staff, the guidance specialist may turn
to a psychologist associated with a child-guidance clinic in the area.
Indeed, any good secondary-school guidance program works closely
with social agencies concerned with employment, health, welfare,

recreation, rehabilitation, community service, and organized youth activities. Some communities achieve close coordination among such agencies, and between them and the school, by means of a specially appointed council.

Guidance specialists also play a central role in the school's external relations. They often provide a placement service for graduates and early leavers who are seeking full-time employment and for students who need part-time jobs. By maintaining close relations with prospective employers they cultivate a source of occupational information and are better able to evaluate the school's curriculum in terms of local needs. Similarly, they solicit evaluative information from the colleges and universities that students attend after graduating from high school.

Counselors also communicate frequently with parents, both in groups and individually. Indeed, there are indications that counseling with selected parents in a group setting may be as beneficial to their children as counseling with the students themselves. Counselors can also help teachers to increase their insight into the problems of students, and thus their effectiveness with them. Through participating in "case conferences" which bring together all the professional people who come in contact with a particular student, teachers can learn much about the forces operating in students' lives that account for their behavior. At these conferences, the teachers contribute information that helps the group to understand the problems of the student in question, and at the same time they learn how the various specialists look at things.

The professional orientation of guidance specialists differs somewhat from that of teachers and administrators. If all three had identical orientations, no differentiation of roles would be necessary or, indeed, possible. All three groups have important roles in carrying out the purposes of the secondary school and must understand and respect one another. Teachers and administrators represent society's interests and function chiefly in a large-group setting. Guidance personnel are primarily oriented to the individual student within that setting, and they deal with students individually. A guidance specialist must, of course, respect societal norms and school requirements, but he must also be prepared to represent an individual student and to espouse a position which conflicts with that of the principal or the faculty. Far from being annoyed by this, administrators and teachers should be grateful for the assurance that the interests of students as individuals are not being overlooked.

## HEALTH AND ATTENDANCE

Regardless of how excellent a secondary-school program is, it is of no value to students when they are absent. Compulsory-education laws require some system of enforcement to assure that students are absent only for acceptable reasons. The "truant officer," once a familiar and formidable figure, has recently been superseded by a professional attendance officer, whose outlook is more like that of a social worker than a policeman. This change reflects the growing emphasis on the individual rather than on the organization, and on causal factors rather than on symptomatic manifestations. The attendance worker knows conditions in many students' homes. Consequently, as a member of the pupil personnel services team, he can help explain the behavior of certain students, participate in decisions affecting them, and cooperate in efforts to help them overcome their difficulties.

In most schools the school nurse investigates absences that may be due to illness, and in some she actually serves as the attendance officer. Although it is useful for the nurse to be familiar with students' home situations, she should not have to leave the health office unattended for long periods of time. Her regular duties are demanding enough: she provides emergency care for students who are injured or become ill in school, examines students seeking readmission after an absence for illness, helps the school physician with medical examinations, determines whether parents have arranged for any treatment their children may need, maintains the health records of students, inspects the school for health and safety hazards, and serves as consultant or instructor in health classes.

This recital of the nurse's tasks suggests three main aspects of the school health program: maintaining a wholesome environment, conducting regular health examinations, and providing systematic instruction. Even those who do not consider the promotion of health a primary goal of secondary education still grant that the school setting ought to be conducive to health and safety, that physical defects of students which interfere with their educational progress ought to be detected and corrected, and that students should have access to the scientific information on which health and safety depend. Teachers contribute to all three aspects. They guard against unhealthful and unsafe conditions and practices in their classrooms; they observe students carefully for signs of illness or handicapping conditions; and some of them participate in health instruction.

REFERRAL SOURCES

The teacher is a specialist in instruction. But in matters of guidance and other student personnel services, he is a "general practitioner." Like the family physician, he is often the first to become aware of a problem that needs attention, and he can turn to a number of specialists for advice.

In order for a system of referral to function effectively, teachers must meet four conditions. First, they must assume that help is available somewhere for any problem that needs attention. Second, they must accept their obligation to the student to locate that help. Third, they must recognize the limits of their own competence so that they will know when referral is appropriate. Finally, they must know what referral resources exist and how to take advantage of them.

Not every problem that arises among students can be solved, of course. There are many matters that we understand so imperfectly that we can do nothing to correct them. There are others that we understand but that we are helpless to alter. Nevertheless, until the teachers and specialists have explored every avenue, they must act as though every problem were capable of being solved. A teacher who merely shrugs and declares a situation hopeless tacitly assumes that no other source of help exists or that if he cannot help, no one else can.

It is even more unfortunate when a teacher knows that help can be found but does not bother to seek it. Such inaction is not necessarily an indication of callousness, however. Secondary-school teachers with heavy work loads and relatively brief contacts with each student are often so busy that they must make a special effort to follow through on a student's difficulty once it has come to their attention. Many problems, of course, go undetected. Moreover, some teachers honestly feel that the personal problems of students are not within the scope of their professional concern nor a legitimate part of the school's responsibility. Yet, while each little difficulty a student has should not be made into a formidable problem, the profession's commitment to learning includes removing, where possible, any impediments to learning.

Once a teacher, for whatever reason, concludes that he is not equipped to provide the help a student seems to need, he should be able to resort to some simple referral procedure. In each school this procedure should be clear. Regardless of the nature of the problem, it is always acceptable to make the referral to the guidance office. The teacher may feel that even the guidance specialist can do nothing about the problem at hand. But he should make the referral anyway. Specialists have their own avenues of referral. But if the teacher fails to make the initial referral, the student may never receive the benefit of the special competence of the nurse, physician, psychologist, psychiatrist, eye doctor, social worker, speech correctionist, reading consultant, physical therapist, dental hygienist, or employment specialist. The secondary-school teacher must realize that teaching is but one of several allied professions which are eager to ensure that students get the maximum benefit from their schooling.

*Suggestions for Class Discussion and Further Investigation*

1. Contrast the responsibility of a classroom teacher for "guidance" in a school that has no guidance specialist on the staff and the responsibility of the teacher in a school in which guidance specialists are available.

2. What help should a teacher be able to expect from a guidance specialist, and what help should the specialist be able to expect from a teacher? Do the two lists consist of complementary functions?

3. Reconstruct your own experiences with guidance personnel when you were in secondary school. What did they do for you that you now recognize as good? What did they do that was not good? What did they not do that you feel they should have done?

4. Assume that a student asked your advice on a personal problem. What would your first utterance in response to his question be? What would your attitude be toward his problem and his asking your advice?

5. Although much time is devoted to the maintaining of students' cumulative records, many teachers seldom refer to them. What information would you want to have readily available? When should cumulative records be consulted—before meeting

a class for the first time, as soon as the teacher knows the class members by name, or only when the need arises in connection with an individual student?

## Suggestions for Further Reading

The literature on guidance and other services is extensive. A good overview is provided by Merle M. Ohlsen in *Guidance Services in the Modern School* (Harcourt, Brace & World, 1964). The place of guidance at the junior-high-school level is discussed in *Junior High School Guidance* by Mauritz Johnson, Jr., William E. Busacker, and Fred Q. Bowman (Harper & Row, 1961).

The counseling approaches of two influential leaders can be compared by examining Carl R. Rogers' *Client-Centered Therapy* (Houghton Mifflin, 1951) and E. G. Williamson's *Counseling Adolescents* (McGraw-Hill, 1950).

Several writers have stressed the teacher's role in guidance. Dugald Arbuckle has discussed this role in *Teacher Counseling* (Addison-Wesley, 1950) and in *Guidance and Counseling in the Classroom* (Allyn and Bacon, 1957). Another source on this topic is *The Role of the Teacher in Guidance,* by Edgar G. Johnston, Mildred Peters, and William Evraiff (Prentice-Hall, 1959).

A good summary of the entire field of student personnel services may be found in Part Two of the 58th Yearbook of the National Society for the Study of Education, *Personnel Services in Education* (University of Chicago Press, 1959). Theoretical questions are considered by C. Gilbert Wrenn in a chapter entitled, "Philosophical and Psychological Bases of Personnel Services in Education," pp. 41–81.

## Chapter Eight

# Instructional Techniques

Every teacher has his own style of teaching, and every subject presents unique instructional problems. Moreover, somewhat different instructional approaches are suitable for learners at various levels of ability and stages of development. It is difficult, therefore, to generalize about instructional techniques in the secondary school. Nevertheless, it is possible to identify a number of problems that are common to all secondary-school teachers, regardless of subject, and that differ somewhat from the problems found at earlier and later levels. In no sense, however, is this discussion intended to supplant the careful examination of methodological problems that every teacher needs to make with respect to his own subject.

Secondary education encompasses a six-year span, and the techniques that are effective with high-school seniors are not entirely appropriate at the junior-high-school level. For good articulation there should be a gradual transition from elementary-school methods to those more appropriate to mature students who are able to assume greater responsibility for their own learning.

The teacher of seventh-graders cannot assume that his pupils have acquired much independence in studying. If they have come from the self-contained classroom of the conventional elementary school, they are accustomed to studying under the close supervision of their teacher. Whatever homework they may have had was assigned only by that same teacher. When the students reach junior high school, they encounter a different teacher for almost every subject. Each has his own standards for performance, and each makes homework assignments with little regard for those being made by other teachers.

Students may also find themselves for the first time in a "study hall," where they are expected to study efficiently without the assistance of a teacher. Many junior high schools have replaced study halls with extended class periods in which students can at least begin their assignments under the supervision of a teacher. Others have tried to control homework by having teachers agree to set a time limit on assignments, or, more artificially, by limiting assignments in each subject to specified days in the week.

Unfortunately, many students make little progress, between the seventh and the twelfth grades, in their ability to study independently. Generally, too much is expected of them in the seventh grade, too little in the twelfth. As a result, they are often distressed by the abrupt change to college standards and procedures. Instruction in the junior high school must include explicit training in how the subjects being taught should be studied. Each teacher is the best authority on how to study his subject. The recently introduced team-teaching approach attempts to make high-school students more responsible for their own learning through provision for independent study and greater use of lectures and other large-group methods.

### INSTRUCTIONAL PLANNING

Whatever methods are used, whether team or individual, systematic instruction requires careful planning. Teachers who undertake to teach a course as a team must plan together with exceptional care. This joint endeavor enables them to pool their ideas on instructional activities and gives inexperienced teachers first-hand experience with skillful planning. In the conventional situation, where each teacher is responsible for his own classes, each must do his own planning. New teachers are often surprised to learn how difficult and time-consuming good instructional planning is. Carrying out a plan effectively requires great skill, but making a good plan in the first place is equally challenging. Planning calls for a high degree of professional judgment as well as imaginativeness. It is perhaps the teacher's most creative act. If he neglects or slights this activity, he can expect his teaching to be desultory and lusterless and his students to be confused, bored, and, perhaps, disorderly. Effective teaching presupposes skillful planning. In planning instruction, a teacher decides exactly how a given group of students will be taught in order to achieve particular learning outcomes.

Curricular planning, which teachers can often do cooperatively, determines what those outcomes should be. In school systems that use state syllabuses, local curricular planning may not occur. Many systems, however, develop their own detailed curriculum guides. These guides or courses of study usually include a list of objectives for the course, an outline of course content, suggestions for learning activities and instructional materials, and illustrative test questions and procedures for evaluation. The use of curriculum guides ensures that each teacher is at least aware of the school policy on what is to be taught, that students in the various sections of a given course taught by several teachers are getting more or less the same instruction, and that there is some continuity from one grade to the next. Neither state syllabuses nor locally developed guides are intended, however, to dictate either the exact order or the precise manner in which the various topics of a course are to be taught. On the other hand, they often serve as a source of ideas which are helpful to a teacher in planning instruction.

Ordinarily, teachers cannot make final decisions regarding the specific content or learning activities of a course until they know the composition of the class they are to teach. Nevertheless, they should have in mind the numerous possibilities from which they can choose. A collection of such possibilities for a major topic is known as a "resource unit." A teacher can prepare his own resource units, join with other teachers in preparing them, or purchase published units. A well-prepared resource unit often suggests instructional approaches and materials that might not be known to a teacher working independently. Resource units are more useful in subjects like social studies and homemaking than in mathematics or foreign languages. In any case, they are extremely time-consuming for an individual teacher to prepare, and those that are published soon get out of date. Therefore, teachers commonly maintain, for each topic, a file folder in which they can keep notes on ideas for classroom activities and information about useful materials.

Resource units deal only with possibilities; lesson plans deal with actualities. Teachers' opinions differ on the place of the lesson in the course. Some teachers regard the daily lesson as a more or less independent entity—related to the ones that precede and follow it, to be sure, but still the basic planning unit of the course. They feel that each lesson should deal with a specific topic, that assignments should be given on a daily basis, and that tests should be scheduled at regular intervals, either weekly or monthly.

Other teachers insist that the course should be divided into fewer, longer instructional units, each encompassing perhaps fifteen to twenty-five lessons. As components of a larger instructional unit, daily lessons are less discrete, and they differ according to whether they are in the initiatory, developmental, or culminating phases of the unit. Advocates of this kind of organization point out that it emphasizes significant relationships rather than isolated bits of knowledge, and that motivation is sustained as each lesson furthers the purposes of the unit. They advocate long-range assignments instead of daily ones, and tests at the completion of each unit rather than at regular time intervals.

A resource unit is a valuable aid in planning an instructional unit for a specific class. The impetus for developing resource units came, however, from a movement during the 1940's and 1950's to involve students in the planning process. To use this approach the teacher must engage in a considerable amount of "pre-planning," which results in a resource unit containing ideas he can suggest to pupils when they are at a loss as to what activities and materials are appropriate.

The rationale for involving students in classroom planning was that they would be more highly motivated to carry out plans they themselves had helped to formulate, that it was important for them to learn how to plan, and that it was democratic to give students some voice in choosing the activities in which they were to engage. In the extreme manifestation of teacher-pupil planning, students help decide not only *how* to approach a topic, but even *what* topics to study. More frequently the teacher presents them with a problem and helps them reach agreement on how they would attack it. Some teachers merely offer students a choice between alternative activities. Most teachers undoubtedly give students no say at all in the matter.

Teachers who are exceptionally skilled in managing groups are very successful at getting students to engage wholeheartedly in planning and in carrying out plans. Others insist that a student is entitled to have his learning activities determined by a professional teacher rather than by his immature classmates. There is little disagreement, though, that whether or not students participate in planning, teachers must motivate them to participate actively in learning activities.

## MOTIVATION AND PARTICIPATION

Some students seem to have little appetite for any learning at all; some seem keener about learning certain subjects than others; and some seem eager to learn anything and everything. It is easy to teach enthusiastic students. Getting reluctant ones to learn what they must learn but have no appetite for is perhaps the greatest challenge in high-school teaching. College teachers, who can assume that most of their students want to learn, usually accept little responsibility for motivating those who do not. Secondary-school teachers, however, need more highly developed instructional skills.

There is no simple way of motivating students to learn. Different students respond differently to the same treatment, and each is motivated by different factors in different situations. What serves as an incentive for one may have no effect on another. For many students high grades are a powerful incentive; for others, who have little hope of attaining them or whose family and friends may actually scoff at such an achievement, grades are an ineffective incentive. Many teachers object that the use of grades as a motivating device distracts students from the real values of learning, and that the fear of failure acts as a negative motivating influence. Nevertheless, as the difficulty of getting into the "right" college increases, extreme grade-consciousness will probably continue to serve as a motivating force among many secondary-school students.

People will work hard at an activity that they think will somehow help them achieve their goals. Secondary teachers often try, therefore, to help students recognize the relation between what they are studying and some vocational goal or some desired personal attainment. Many students, of course, lack well-defined goals, and not everyone would agree that a strictly utilitarian value should be ascribed to much that is learned in school. To view each course primarily as a prerequisite for another rather than as important in its own right is to carry the propaedeutic emphasis too far.

Another way of using goals to motivate students is to focus attention on the immediate learning enterprise. Thus, the completion of the task at hand—an instructional unit or a project, for example—may elicit the energies of students even when they are not conscious of the learning they are deriving from the activity. Some teachers argue that permitting students to share in planning classroom activities commits them to pursue the purposes they adopt. Such camouflaging of the true purposes of learning activities, may, however, weaken students' desire to acquire learning for its own sake. Engaging students in purposeful participation is desirable if their purpose is to learn. Otherwise, it may distract them from the real business at hand in much the same way that teachers' efforts to sugar-coat learning creates the impression that learning is always easy and pleasant.

The most widely accepted theory of motivation makes use of the construct of "needs." When, through deprivation or arousal, a primary physiological or secondary psychological need makes itself felt, the individual is impelled to behave in some way. He supposedly engages in behavior directed at some goal-object or condition which he perceives as having the potential of satisfying or reducing the need. This theory helps high-school teachers understand why students fall asleep in class, why they are listless immediately before lunch, and why they hold hands in the corridors. It also predicts that students will at various times and in various ways seek attention and recognition (or approval). They will strive for a sense of security and adequacy (or achievement), and a feeling of acceptance and belonging among their contemporaries. Understanding these things may give a teacher clues to the best approach to use with an individual student, but it does little to help him stimulate the learning of all the students in a classroom. In group instruction, the theory is of some value if it reminds the teacher that tasks which are too difficult or too easy for students do not lead to a sense of achievement but to a sense of frustration or ennui, that encouragement and praise are more effective than criticism and rebuke, and that adolescents derive satisfaction from working together in groups.

Some individuals have a greater need to achieve and excel, some are more insecure, and some crave more attention. These differences are presumably due to previous experiences, especially in the home. During adolescence, other individual differences increase. Specific mental abilities become more sharply delineated and students develop special interests. Those who are strong in one subject may be weak in another, and their interests may not always coincide with their abilities. The selection of course content or learning tasks on the basis of common "needs" or interests, even if it were desirable, is next to impossible at the secondary-school level.

Developing interest in learning is a goal in itself, quite apart from its motivational value. Most teachers want their students to learn their subject and to become interested in it as well. But no subject is inherently interesting or uninteresting. The problem is not "making a subject interesting" but arousing students' interest in learning it. Still, while students find it easier to learn when they are interested, they must expect to have to learn much when they are not. Fortunately, a student who originally engages in an activity because he is required to tends to continue it on his own volition even when he is no longer required to do so. Presumably this autonomy of interest comes about because the activity satisfies some basic need in the individual. Learning is itself satisfying.

Interest implies active participation in a learning task. Passivity in learning has long been condemned, but activity has long been misconstrued. In the instructional situation of the secondary school, activity refers to reading, discussing, organizing, analyzing, comparing, deducing, discovering, interpreting, and the like rather than to physical movement, construction, or the carrying out of "projects." Teachers must be sure that the interest they stimulate is in activities inherent in the learning process. Irrelevant activities, such as playing games and participating in situations contrived to be lifelike, may have temporary appeal for students, but they are not sound bases for motivation. Likewise, students' existing interests may serve as starting points for engaging them in learning activities, but in the long run the teacher is better off relying on their curiosity, their desire to know, and their inclination to make sense out of the universe and to impose order upon it.

To interest students is to intrigue them. This is the underlying motivational assumption of the curriculum reform movement, which emphasizes discovery and inquiry within the context of a disciplinary structure. What intrigues is that which is unexpected, unexplained, surprising, puzzling, incongruous—a discrepancy between what is known or believed and what is confronted. Festinger[1] calls the mental effect of such discrepancy "cognitive dissonance." Piaget[2] speaks of "equilibration," whereby the individual's cognitive structure must either be able to "assimilate" new information or be altered so as to "accommodate" it. Gardner Murphy's[3] phrase "the urge to understand" seems to express a similar idea, and Jerome Bruner's[4] "competence motive" suggests a need to master the novel and challenging. Because what is familiar is seldom intriguing,

[1] Leon Festinger, "The Motivating Effect of Cognitive Dissonance," in Robert J. C. Harper, *et al.*, eds., *The Cognitive Processes*, Prentice-Hall, 1964, pp. 509–38.

[2] Jean Piaget, *Psychology of Intelligence*, Littlefield, Adams, 1960, pp. 6–8; also, *Piaget Revisited*, Verne Rockcastle and Richard E. Ripple, eds., School of Education, Cornell University, 1964.

[3] Gardner Murphy, "Nonrational Processes in Learning," in *The Revolution in Our Schools*, Ronald Gross and Judith Murphy, eds., Harcourt, Brace & World, 1964, pp. 157–69.

[4] Jerome Bruner, "The Act of Discovery," in *On Knowing*, Belknap Press, 1962, p. 89.

Phenix[5] argues that content relating to ordinary life situations has less motivational appeal than content from the scholarly disciplines.

## PRESENTATION AND DISCOVERY

At any given hour of the school day there is likely to be a different activity under way in every classroom of the typical American secondary school. For each subject certain methods of instruction are more appropriate than others. And in the teaching of each subject different goals call for different techniques. Resourceful teachers try to accommodate individual differences among students by using a variety of learning activities and materials. Moreover, they know that an occasional change of pace quickens motivation by dispelling monotony and listlessness, especially at the junior-high-school level, where the interest span of students is relatively short.

Nevertheless, excessive variety merely for the sake of variety may create a confusion and insecurity that are as disruptive as the boredom produced by the lack of variety. Students derive a certain reassurance from established routines and familiar procedures. The teacher's goal, therefore, is a moderate and purposeful variation in his approach. Achieving it demands of him more creativity and better planning than does the use of the same activities day after day.

Some mathematics teachers fall into the pattern of having students write the homework on the blackboard every day, "going over" each problem, presenting new material, and assigning more homework with which to begin the cycle the next day. Similarly, teachers of other subjects habitually limit classroom activities to oral recitations on assigned reading, followed mechanically by the giving out of another reading assignment. Even the teacher who has his students work in committees at every class meeting is as guilty of monotonous instruction as the one who constantly lectures.

Beginning teachers, perhaps because of their recent college experience, tend to rely too heavily on lectures in the secondary school. Some educators seem convinced that the lecture has no place at all at that level. They observe that telling is not teaching, and they conclude that teaching cannot involve telling. Poor lectures, of course, have no place at any level, and a good lecture accompanied by demonstrations and visual projections takes far more time to prepare than is generally realized. Furthermore, the lecture is appropriate only for certain purposes; it is no substitute for drill, discussion, refer-

[5] Philip Phenix, *Realms of Meaning*, McGraw-Hill, 1964, p. 346.

ence reading, creative activity, or heuristic questioning. Lectures for junior-high-school students should be briefer and less frequent than for more mature students, and the teacher should take time at the outset to teach students how to listen and how to take notes properly. The teacher who trains students to benefit from lectures will find that he can use this instructional device more frequently.

Any activity that does not depend for its effectiveness on interaction, manipulation, or individual coaching can probably be carried out most efficiently in large-group situations. Only recently have schools begun to explore ways of using instructional groups of a hundred or more students. By presenting lectures, showing films, and giving tests to large groups like this, the school can free time for teachers to use for planning and preparation and can afford to set up small discussion groups of ten to fifteen students. Moreover, the large-group arrangement makes it unnecessary for the teacher or a guest speaker to repeat a lecture several times.

For years teachers have been urged to use local residents with special knowledge or skills as "resource people" for class instruction, and to take students on field trips to various places. When community resources offer educational opportunities that cannot be duplicated in any other way, they should certainly be incorporated into the program of instruction. The trouble is that using them is often more trouble than they are worth. Even when inadequate planning does not make them downright worthless, greater benefits can often be derived from other approaches. Nevertheless, many teachers make judicious use of such resources to culminate a unit of study, to illustrate a concept vividly, or to provide information not readily available from other sources.

Audio-visual techniques, if improperly used, can also lead to the squandering of valuable time. But they are at least more convenient for the teacher to use and far easier to control. Selective judgment is essential here because, though some audio-visual materials are of excellent quality, some are poor—technically, intellectually, and pedagogically. Some, like those prepared by several science curriculum committees, are tailor-made for a particular course, whereas many others used in schools are only peripherally related to what is being studied. Printed materials, including textbooks, also vary in quality and relevance, but textbooks are usually carefully chosen, and the use of related reading matter usually does not usurp the instructional time of a whole class. Audio-visual materials can easily be regarded as entertainment by the class or merely provide a respite for the teacher.

Two assumptions underlying the use of field trips and multi-sensory teaching aids are that direct experience is always superior to vicarious experience and that instruction should always be as concrete as possible. But the ability to deal with abstract ideas is an important instructional goal in secondary schools. One might argue, therefore, that students should operate at an abstraction level which is as high as possible but as low as necessary and that they should increasingly be expected to learn from vicarious experience. Sheer verbalization devoid of meaning is, of course, to be avoided. But words and symbols carry ideas more effectively than pictures or objects.

Teachers use demonstrations and such sensory aids as charts, projections, and recordings primarily to supplant or enhance the lectures as a means of exposition. Expository presentations seek to inform, explain, or put before students material that they are to learn or evaluate. Teachers often have students make such presentations to the class. Undoubtedly, a student learns a great deal about a topic while preparing his presentation, and he probably profits from presenting it to his classmates. But how much the classmates learn is another question and one that merits careful consideration by the teacher who uses this technique excessively.

In quite another form of presentation, the teacher elicits responses from the class instead of dispensing information and ideas. In a discussion the students' responses are reactions to the questions and statements of both the teacher and other students. The teacher must have questions ready but he should encourage students to use their own. Skillfully led, a discussion can lead to valid conclusions or at least to an awareness that opinions differ.

Much time can be wasted exchanging uninformed opinions. In developmental teaching, there is little opinion-laden interchange among students. Instead, skillful questioning by the teacher enables students to discover meanings and generalizations by thinking correctly about the facts available to them. Unlike the questions used in a discussion to stimulate divergent thinking, the questions are used heuristically to produce convergent thinking which proceeds step by step to a desired conclusion. The teacher must plan the questioning as carefully as he plans an expository presentation, but the specific direction the heuristic takes is determined by each response students make. The laboratory method in its best form similarly makes use of a heuristic leading to the discovery of empirical truths through manipulation, observation, and measurement. Though best suited to mathematics and science, variations in this discovery approach can promote active learning in many other fields. As Bruner has pointed out, the student must be helped to develop a heuristic of his own with which to attack problems independently.

Sometimes the procedure of having students look for information in various references is erroneously considered illustrative of the discovery method. In the so-called group problem-solving method, students commonly gather facts and share their findings with the others in the group. Consulting a variety of books and pamphlets for information is not discovery but recovery. In this case, printed materials are merely substituting for the teacher or the textbook as a source of information. Discovery has to do with thinking rather than with data-gathering, with finding or figuring things out for oneself, rather than with consulting authorities.

Problem-solving is an excellent learning activity if the problems are worth solving and if they can be solved. In many instances, what passes for problem-solving in secondary-school classrooms meets neither of these conditions, and the problems are in fact not solved, though they may be examined and discussed. Students should not get the impression that collating facts from a number of sources is problem-solving or that consensus among a group of adolescents constitutes a solution.

It is essential that students learn how to find desired information in library sources. But to use such sources exclusively as a primary means of getting facts is too time-consuming. It is quite appropriate for the teacher to present information to students orally or through documents, so long as he also helps them to develop concepts and to discover for themselves generalizations, principles, rules, and other relationships among concepts.

Critical thinking is not the same as problem-solving. Ennis[6] has defined critical thinking as "the correct assessing of statements." This assessment involves such operations as grasping meaning, defining, finding assumptions, noting ambiguities and contradictions, and judging whether conclusions necessarily follow, whether observations are reliable, and whether a given principle is applied. From

6 Robert H. Ennis, "A Concept of Critical Thinking," *Harvard Educational Review*, 32 (Winter 1962), pp. 81–111.

observations of classroom discourse, Smith[7] has found that teachers also engage in other linguistic behaviors: classifying, explaining, conditional inferring, comparing and contrasting, valuating, and designating. It is through performing such logical operations on subject matter that students learn how to think. They can participate just as actively in performing these operations as in carrying out group projects or engaging in cooperative problem-solving activities.

The effectiveness of a secondary-school teacher lies not in whether or not he lectures, or permits group activities, or conducts practice drills, or leads discussions, or develops understanding heuristically, but in whether he does skillfully whichever of these is appropriate for achieving a given outcome with the students he is teaching.

## HOMEWORK

The chief contacts parents have with their children's school are through homework and report cards. Most secondary-school teachers and most parents attach considerable importance to homework. Only occasionally do people ask whether or not there should be homework; most frequently they ask how much there should be or what kind is best.

School policies on the amount of homework that teachers may assign must take into account differences among both subjects and grades. Younger students, at least, should be helped to begin their assignments in class. A successful start increases the likelihood of their finishing the work later. Possibly the two greatest problems for teachers regarding homework are getting students to do it and evaluating it when they do.

It is difficult enough for a teacher to induce a student to do something when the student is physically present; it is far more difficult when the student is elsewhere, under someone else's control. Experienced teachers realize that homework is not entirely within their control, and they do not get upset when some students do not get it done. Most high-school students are conscientious about doing assignments, sometimes so much so that they endanger both their health and family harmony. The school should give parents some idea of how much time students are expected to spend on homework in order that they may cooperate in seeing that their children neither neglect it nor spend a disproportionate amount of time on it. Often

---

[7] B. Othanel Smith, "A Concept of Teaching," in B. O. Smith and R. H. Ennis, eds., *Language and Concepts in Education*, Rand McNally, 1961, pp. 86–101.

students can proceed with an assignment with a little outside help. Instead of telling parents not to interfere, schools should encourage them to help their children if they can, without doing the work for them.

Whether students will do their assignments and profit from doing them depends to a large extent on the appropriateness of the assignments. An assignment is appropriate if students understand its purpose, have access to needed materials, and possess the skills needed to carry it out. Thus, teachers should tell students what they are expected to learn from a reading assignment. Too often students are merely told to read the next ten pages in the textbook or to find the answers to the questions at the end of a chapter. In assigning students to investigate a topic in a number of sources, teachers must remember that many students do not have encyclopedias or other reference books in their homes and cannot readily get to a library. Creative activities, such as writing and drawing, often make suitable assignments because they allow for differences in students' abilities. In general, assignments should give students practice in using skills or operations that they have already learned rather than in using new ones that they have to learn by themselves. All students in a class do not always need the same kind and amount of practice, however. Various subgroups can be given different assignments.

Daily assignments are important in such subjects as mathematics and foreign languages, whereas in others longer-range assignments are often preferable. In the junior high school, teachers find it necessary to check periodically to see what progress students are making with an extended assignment. Lengthy term papers should be reserved for more mature and capable students, and even then they should be used sparingly in the secondary school.

To some extent the nature of the assignment suggests how the student's performance should be evaluated. The teacher should acknowledge the completion of homework whenever possible, even if he does not check its content. Often he should call the student's attention to errors and require him to correct them. With complex exercises, such as the writing of compositions, the teacher can avoid undermining the student's confidence by concentrating on a few types of error at a time, instead of noting his every shortcoming.

Although lengthy term papers should probably be assigned infrequently in the secondary school, such lengthy assignments usually call for achievement of a kind that cannot be evaluated through examinations. The student is entitled to receive a grade for such achievement. On the other hand, daily exercises that are intended to strengthen skills or improve retention need not be marked. The results of students' efforts on these assignments will show up on tests. Many teachers collect such homework only occasionally; ordinarily they merely check it in class for completeness and discuss any points that need clarification.

## EVALUATION

The teacher's success in the planning and presentation phases of instruction is revealed when he evaluates students' achievement. Only an extremely unperceptive teacher would attribute disappointing results entirely to the shortcomings of his students and not at all to his own teaching. It may be, as Henry Adams suggested, that a teacher affects eternity, but surely he is accountable for some more immediate effects as well.

The results of learning can be detected only indirectly, through some kind of performance—oral, written, or manual—on the part of the learner. To determine how well a student has learned a skill, the teacher usually requires him to demonstrate it. The teacher can check on the acquisition of factual knowledge rather easily through oral or written questions. He can test the understanding of concepts and generalizations through carefully designed examination items. Much more difficult to assess are such outcomes as changes in attitudes, the growth of esthetic appreciation, and the ability to make interpretations, analyses, syntheses, and applications.

It is unfortunate that we tend to associate evaluation mainly with marks and promotion. All too often students are more concerned with passing tests than with learning, and are more interested in the marks they receive than in knowing where they need to improve. Nevertheless, the emphasis on "measuring" achievement quantitatively rather than on describing it qualitatively has undoubtedly helped make students mark-conscious. Teachers can mitigate the emphasis on marks somewhat by giving greater attention to the diagnostic function of tests and less to their use as over-all assessments of achievement. By analyzing the errors students make on tests, a teacher can both identify weaknesses in his teaching and determine what remedial experiences individual students need.

It is usually not possible to use end-of-course examinations diagnostically. Nevertheless, like unit tests, they stimulate students to pull together relationships among component learnings. Students get a better understanding of material learned in the earlier stages of a unit or course when they review it in the light of subsequent learnings. However, since examinations tend to suggest what learnings are considered most significant, teachers must be sure that their tests do in fact reflect the important objectives rather than trivial ones. Constructing good examinations and analyzing the results is extremely time-consuming. Giving examinations too frequently tends to compromise their quality. In addition, it puts students in the position of spending more time in preparing for and taking tests than in engaging in more fruitful learning activities.

In certain subjects, however, teachers find that giving frequent brief quizzes, often of a factual nature, motivates students and identifies their difficulties. If the answers are discussed immediately, correct responses are reinforced. Often teachers do not record marks on such quizzes. Still, the accumulation of marks from many such short tests results in an assessment of achievement which is probably more reliable than one based on homework marks.

The questions on quizzes are usually of the short-answer type. Indeed, secondary-school teachers use objective-type items on most examinations, because they permit a wide sampling of course material and can be scored more objectively and quickly than can essays. Moreover, teachers can readily determine how difficult each such item is and how well it discriminates between better and poorer students. Teachers who maintain a pool of tested items are able to devise more and more effective tests. Nevertheless, objective tests cannot evaluate all kinds of learning outcomes with equal effectiveness. The essay type is more appropriate for testing a student's ability to express ideas, synthesize data, and construct logical arguments. Both types are often used together in an examination. Since students tend to prepare somewhat differently for each type, they review more comprehensively when the two are combined. Occasionally, a check list, a rating scale, or an inventory is a more suitable evaluative device than any kind of test. In evaluating, as in planning, teachers must have clearly in mind what it is they are trying to do. The outcomes that are evaluated must be the same as those that guided the planning.

*Suggestions for Class Discussion and Further Investigation*

1. Analyze the process of studying. Can pupils be taught to study, or must they learn to study without the benefit of instruction? Would your own subject be taught differently by a teacher

who considered it part of his responsibility to teach pupils how to study the subject? In what respects?

2. Contrast the instructional techniques appropriate to the elementary school with those appropriate to the senior high school by listing the variables and indicating the nature of the change between the two levels. Is the combination of the two necessary at the junior-high-school level? Is the difference between techniques suitable for slow learners and able students similar to the difference between techniques suitable for younger children and older adolescents?

3. Would you prefer to teach independently, or as a member of a team? What advantages and disadvantages does team-teaching seem to have?

4. During the 1940's and 1950's much emphasis was placed on "teacher-pupil planning." To what extent should students participate in deciding on learning activities? To what extent in determining goals?

5. From your own experience as a student, analyze what makes a subject or an activity interesting or uninteresting. Is anything inherently interesting or uninteresting, or is interest entirely a subjective reaction? Can teachers "make" a subject interesting? Should they try to? Does it help a teacher to understand "basic human needs" and the "interests of adolescents"?

6. Some teachers disdain the gadgetry of audio-visual devices and the so-called "newer instructional media." Others make extensive use of these aids in their teaching. How do you account for this extreme difference in attitude? Is the usefulness of these materials more a function of the subject being taught, or of the personality of the teacher?

7. How do some teachers stifle creativity among their pupils? How do some teachers foster it? In general, is too much emphasis placed in our secondary schools upon convergent rather than divergent thinking? Does an emphasis upon "critical thinking" inhibit "creative thinking"? What are the relative values of critical and creative thinking in your subject field?

8. List some examples of "good" and "poor" homework assignments. Generalize the characteristics to be sought in assignments.

9. Write one good multiple-choice question in your subject field

and then write one good essay question on the same topic. Which took more time?

*Suggestions for Further Reading*

One of the volumes prepared by the National Education Association's Project on Instruction is *Planning and Organizing for Teaching* (National Education Association, 1963), by John Goodlad. The content of this book is summarized in Chapter 3 of *Schools for the Sixties* (National Education Association, 1963), pp. 63–108.

One of the most influential recent books on the subject of instruction is the report of the Woods Hole Conference by Jerome S. Bruner, *The Process of Education* (Harvard University Press, 1960). Bruner's essay on "The Act of Discovery" appears both in his book, *On Knowing* (Belknap Press, 1962), and in *The Revolution in the Schools,* edited by Ronald Gross and Judith Murphy (Harcourt, Brace & World, 1964), pp. 145–56. The latter publication also includes Gardner Murphy's "Nonrational Process of Learning," pp. 157–69.

A volume of great significance is the *Handbook of Research on Teaching,* edited by N. L. Gage (Rand McNally, 1963). The research on the teaching of various subjects is reviewed by authorities in the respective fields: social studies by Lawrence E. Metcalf; composition and literature by Henry C. Merkel; mathematics by Kenneth B. Henderson; science by Fletcher G. Watson; foreign languages by John B. Carroll; and the visual arts by Jerome Hansman. Students will be interested in the discussions of their own subjects, but of interest to all is Harry S. Broudy's essay in Chapter 1, entitled "Historic Exemplars of Teaching Method."

Another recent volume with contributions by leading educational psychologists is Part I of the 63rd Yearbook of the National Society for the Study of Education, *Theories of Learning and Instruction,* edited by Ernest R. Hilgard (University of Chicago Press, 1964). Included are chapters on motivation by Pauline S. Sears, on readiness by Fred T. Tyler, on creative thinking and problem-solving by Jacob W. Getzels, on theories of teaching by N. L. Gage, on the educational reform movements by Paul Woodring, on some instructional theorems by Jerome S. Bruner, on reading by John B. Carroll, and on programed learning by Sidney L. Pressey and by A. A. Lumsdaine.

## Chapter Nine

# Management and Control

No high-school teacher likes to think of himself as an "organization man." Yet however much a teacher may wish to be left alone to teach his subject and to work with growing minds and developing personalities, he must inevitably face a variety of less-inspiring institutional demands. Even a private tutor has some "housekeeping" chores to perform. But when a teacher chooses to practice his profession in an organized school, he assumes certain responsibilities for the management and control of that school. True, the administrative, clerical, and maintenance staffs take on most of that job. And improved institutional arrangements promise to relieve the teacher of some of the routine tasks he is currently expected to perform. But the fact remains that the progress of pupils through school, as well as their conduct in it, must be regulated; instructional materials must be selected and used; and "school must keep."

## SCHOOL ROUTINES

Some administrators seem to be more interested in straight window shades than in straight thinking, more impressed by neat bulletin boards than by creative teaching, more concerned about the promptness with which teachers file reports than about the soundness of their scholarship. And it must be said that many teachers also are overly concerned about orderliness, neatness, and promptness. Understandably, the teacher who is an exteme nonconformist and who delights in flouting convention irritates even the most enlightened administrator. Nor is there any particular virtue in disorder. The best administration is unobtrusive, but the careless, heedless, or uncooperative teacher obtrudes upon arrangements that are designed to make the school run smoothly and effectively.

Routines require neither thought nor creativity. Consequently, they free time for thoughtful and creative endeavors. The teacher can gain even more time by having students help with classroom routines. Such activity benefits the students as well, by increasing their sense of responsibility and by satisfying their need for recognition. Many beginning teachers do not realize, and some experienced teachers have never learned, that they have many willing hands available. In most well-run industrial arts shops the teacher rotates assignments for various cleaning-up and tool-accounting tasks. Homerooms and libraries commonly enlist the aid of volunteer helpers. Since home chores are pretty much a thing of the past, assigning them at school gives students a chance to feel useful.

Some chores obviously cannot be delegated to students. Attendance registers are legal documents; many reports are official in nature; and the requisitioning of materials requires professional judgment. Nor should students be deprived of valuable study time to furnish "slave labor" for routine duties. But there are numerous short waiting periods in every school day when students can easily contribute to the functioning and appearance of their school. In almost every period of the day, students can gain added instructional time by expediting some necessary classroom maneuver. They can, for example, collect and distribute materials, fetch and return stored articles, erase boards, water plants, dust shelves, arrange bulletin boards, greet visitors, carry messages, police the floor, align furniture, operate projectors, and maintain certain records. Five minutes saved during each class meeting can add the equivalent of a month of instruction to the school year; a similar saving during each of six periods each day can give every student an additional semester of secondary education. Growth cannot be hurried, and assembly-line standards are not appropriate for education. And yet undue casualness and chronic inefficiency only detract from learning.

## DISCIPLINE

A discourse on discipline is an exercise in futility. No set of directions, no list of rules, can teach a person how to get other people to do what he wishes them to do. Yet without discipline there cannot be effective teaching. And, significantly, without effective teaching good classroom discipline is hard to achieve.

Discipline is more difficult to maintain in the secondary school than it is at any other educational level. The elementary school deals in the main with children who, despite their lack of socialization, are physically small enough to be manageable. The college deals with students whose motivation and maturity dispose them to observe adult rules of conduct, at least when they are in class. But the secondary school cannot maintain social control by relying on either childish docility or adult earnestness. Some of the students are in school against their will; many are more responsive to the code of their fellow students than to the symbols of adult authority; and most are at one stage or another in the process of asserting themselves as individuals. Junior-high-school students in particular are often boisterous, silly, moody, and given to extreme reactions and vacillating behavior. Predictably unpredictable, they chafe under rigidly consistent treatment; yet they are confused by inconsistency. Though they seem to be rebelling against adult authority, they are rebelling even more against childhood and are striving desperately to achieve adulthood. If they seem to be trying to see what they "can get away with," in reality they are continually experimenting with a new role and for the first time are having to accommodate almost hourly to the expectations of a number of different teachers. Sometimes they simply forget or misjudge what is and what is not acceptable in a particular teacher's classroom. As they are trying to adapt to a variety of teacher personalities and are groping toward an altered status, they are at the same time bewildered by the changing attitudes and reactions of classmates who are developing unevenly around them.

Most secondary-school teachers understand the phenomenon of adolescence in our culture. But it is one thing to understand adolescent behavior and quite another to accept it and to know how to cope with it. There are many situations in which nobody would know for certain what was best to do, and there are some in which no possible action is likely to be very effective. Teachers who expect a complete absence of conflict in human relations doom themselves to disappointment and to feelings of guilt and inadequacy.

Discipline cannot be imposed, nor is it suddenly acquired. It is learned slowly. And it is a complex learning, continually modified, and characterized by numerous trials, errors, and corrected responses. A teacher and his colleagues are not merely *maintaining* discipline; they are in effect *teaching* it. And they are doing so during only a few of the student's waking hours, often in the face of strong countervailing influences. With some students a teacher may be gratified by even a barely noticeable improvement in conduct during a school year. Indeed, considering the circumstances under which some students live, the school has done well if it has prevented them from becoming even less amenable to social control.

Beginning teachers would do well to realize that the problem of discipline is one that teachers can learn to handle but can never rid themselves of. Experienced teachers can tell what approaches they have found effective, but the effectiveness of the approaches probably lies in what the teachers learned in the process of discovering them. They cannot be handed down. Furthermore, there is no assurance that what works for one teacher will work for another. It makes a difference whether the teacher is male or female, elderly or young, large or small, vivacious or reserved, worried or relaxed, tired or rested, ill or healthy. It makes a difference whether the subject is required or elective, whether the class is bright or dull, whether it is early morning or late afternoon, winter or spring, Tuesday or Friday, stormy or sunny.

Still, despite all the variables, some teachers do learn how to handle discipline and others do not. Those who learn make greater use of analysis than of brawn or impulse. Some things are obvious. Evasion, for example, *seems* to solve problems but actually aggravates them. There are times when the teacher must turn to someone else for help in dealing with a pupil. But the student who is sent to the principal eventually returns to the classroom, and the teacher's problem is still unresolved if not intensified.

Some educators are fond of saying that behavior is caused. It undoubtedly is. But it is also complex, and so are its causes. A teacher can, in any given situation, only hope to surmise what some of those causes might be, and even then he must be content to deal with only a few of them. Nevertheless, the rational thing to do is to try to understand what causes are operative.

Extremes in treatment seem to cause undesirable behavior. One student may incessantly seek attention because overindulgence at home has led him to expect that he will always be the center of attention and will always have his own way. Another student may seek attention because neglect or indifference at home has led him to strive for what he craves by doing things that he knows will be noticed. A student who is not challenged by his school work becomes bored and tries to relieve his boredom. A student for whom the work is too challenging becomes frustrated and strikes out against his tormentors or seeks satisfactions in fantasy or illicit activities.

Teachers and enlightened parents have been made so conscious of mental health that they sometimes interpret every antisocial act as an indication of sickness for which the perpetrator cannot be held responsible. Every student who is quiet or who prefers solitude is seen as "withdrawn," and adolescent horseplay is either condoned as "acting-out behavior" or deplored as "overaggression."

Labels for behavior are not very helpful. Nevertheless, while a teacher cannot be expected to be a clinician, he should be able to identify students who need to be referred to a counselor for help. In the long run the behavior of some children may be redirected through a combination of skillful counseling and intelligent handling in the classroom. But secondary-school teachers cannot neglect the immediate situation while waiting for the ultimate solution.

Both the school setting and the situation in each classroom have an effect on discipline. It is obvious that good discipline produces an atmosphere throughout the school and within each classroom which allows instruction and other activities to proceed efficiently. It is less obvious that the behavior of an individual depends in part on the group situation in which he finds himself. Even students who are usually well behaved find it difficult to avoid unacceptable conduct in a deteriorating group situation. The first step in achieving discipline, then, is to establish and maintain a wholesome setting in which difficulties are unlikely to arise. This "strategic prevention" supplements "tactical prevention," by which an alert and prudent teacher forestalls untoward incidents moment by moment in the classroom. The more successful these two types of prevention are, the less need there is for the third kind of action, which is corrective in nature.

In American secondary schools adults have entered into a partnership with students in an effort to give them a proprietary interest in their schools and to encourage in them a sense of responsibility. Student government enables students to help formulate and interpret the rules that are essential to well-ordered institutional life. Teachers act as interested advisers in the students' own activity programs. The curriculum is adapted to individual characteristics. Instruction, when carefully planned and skillfully executed, provides varied experiences in which students are kept actively engaged and are given reasonable opportunities for success. It is not these specific measures in themselves, but rather the underlying feeling of mutual respect and confidence between faculty and students, that prevents discipline problems.

But the realistic teacher still realizes that he must take certain positive steps to prevent disorder in the classroom. Sophisticated teachers observe what is taking place and use sound judgment in deciding when to overlook a given action and when to nip it in the bud. Most classes in secondary schools are conducted informally, with the give and take of easy discussion, the noise that accompanies productive activity, and reasonable freedom of movement. But in order for students to learn that discourse must be kept germane and polite and that movement and noise must not be disturbing, they need the assurance that the teacher will remind them when they are in danger of overstepping the limits of acceptability. Most adolescents appreciate a teacher who refuses to let them get away with what they know they should not do. They also appreciate a teacher who comes close enough to speak to them quietly instead of shouting hysterically, who gives fair warning instead of idle threats, and who adroitly shifts the class activity or engages an incipient miscreant in some constructive task before trouble arises.

When trouble does arise, as it inevitably must, the teacher's choice of corrective action is circumscribed both by law and by moral principles and common sense. Corporal methods of punishment are proscribed by some states and school systems, but even when permitted the propriety of a teacher's striking a girl and the wisdom of his taking on a boy larger than himself are at best questionable. For practical purposes, corporal punishment must be reserved for use with small boys by those teachers who cannot exercise control in a more persuasive and rational manner.

In any case, the teacher must consider the welfare of both the group and the offender, and both the requirements of the immediate situation and the eventual rehabilitation of the offender. Punishment should be both appropriate and effective. To be appropriate it should be commensurate in severity with the seriousness of the offense and, if possible, it should be a natural consequence of the offense. Thus, restitution is a logical punishment for damage or theft of property, and abuse of privileges should result in their temporary loss. Only in schools where students have many privileges is it feasible to withhold a privilege. The effectiveness of punishment can be gauged by noting how often an offense recurs. Schools that use "detention rooms" might note, for example, whether the number of offenders diminishes throughout the school year and whether the same students repeatedly appear as offenders. The only offense for which detaining students after school is a logical consequence is tardiness, as a result of which time was lost earlier in the day.

Detention periods, in any case, are subject to misinterpretation by students, especially when no clear distinction is made between detention for punishment and detention for remedial help. When teachers are willing to furnish help after school hours, students should accept it willingly and appreciatively and should not confuse opportunity with penance. But if school work is required of students who are detained for punitive reasons, an erroneous and distasteful view of supplementary work arises in the minds of all the students. This danger is also present when a teacher assigns additional homework to an unruly class or requires a troublesome student to write a composition on his responsibilities or on the error of his ways. The same principle applies to the unjustifiable practice of lowering pupils' marks as punishment. Students should view assignments and marks as related to learning and achievement, not to conduct.

## MARKING AND PROMOTION

The placement of students while they are in school, their eventual graduation, and their subsequent success in being selected for occupational or further educational opportunities all hinge on a system of marking through which teachers indicate their evaluation of students' achievement. In effect, society has assigned to the secondary school a selection or screening function which enables it to determine to a large degree the fate of each student. Therefore, marks are of great importance to each individual, whether he cares about them or not.

The marking system used in a school must be based on an explicit, consistent marking policy which is at least adhered to, if not subscribed to, by all the members of the faculty. Academic freedom does not imply that each teacher has the right to mark idiosyncratically. True, complete consistency among teachers is unattainable, but teachers who are aware of the seriousness of the problem can achieve *reasonable* consistency so long as they know what the school's marking policy is.

No single system of marking can serve several mutually incompatible purposes. One purpose—the descriptive-predictive—is based on the assumption that marks which accurately describe a student's achievement in school are helpful in predicting his subsequent performance. Thus, marks enter into decisions regarding employment, acceptance for further education, and eligibility for scholarship awards. If the marks were devised in the first place for a completely different purpose, all these decisions will be based on an unfounded assumption.

A second purpose for which marks are commonly used is to provide motivation. Descriptive-predictive marks serve as powerful motivators for some students, primarily those with the ability and encouragement to achieve high ones. The fear of failing a course or getting lower marks than are expected of them also serves as a negative form of motivation for some. But some students can seldom earn passing marks, to say nothing of high ones. In an effort to extend the motivational effects to all students, therefore, some teachers have adopted the practice of basing marks on the extent to which students do their best or achieve up to their apparent ability. Since a student's best may be none too good, marks assigned on this basis have little predictive value. Moreover, since the student himself probably knows whether he is doing his best, it is not particularly useful to tell him whether or not the teacher shares his opinion.

A third kind of marking is diagnostic in nature. Here marks serve to focus attention on the relative strengths and weaknesses in a student's performance, rather than on comparing its over-all quality with that of other students or with the student's own potential. Although such diagnostic, or analytical, marking is rare, it is the most useful of all, because it gives the student guidance on the specific aspects of his work that need attention. Two students may each receive "C" at some point in a course for quite different reasons, and they may need to perform entirely different learning tasks to improve their over-all performance.

Obviously a single mark cannot serve all three of these purposes. That is why a good many schools use more than one system. They may use different symbols for each set of marks, or else superscripts or different-colored inks. Both for immediate communication and for correct interpretation when records are later consulted in the making of decisions, the basis for marks must be clear. Some kinds of performance can be described fairly objectively. For example, a teacher can describe a student's typing ability in terms of words per minute and number of errors per page, and he can describe the quality of a student's handwriting by scaling it against a standard chart. But ordinarily the only way a teacher can indicate the quality of a student's over-all achievement is to compare it with the achievement of other students. Clearly, the significance of a mark depends on who those other students are.

If we know something about the composition of a particular class, then it may be informative for us to know how a given student's performance ranks with respect to the performance of the other students in the class. If we know something about the standing of a school among schools across the state or nation, then it may be informative for us to know how a given student's performance compares with that of others in his grade, assuming that the grade itself is fairly typical of grades in the school. Comparison within a class is, of course, the easiest kind of comparison for a teacher to make; in order to compare with a whole grade, some sort of common examination must be used, even if the curriculum is modified for some sections of the grade.

In a state like New York, where external examinations are given in specific subjects, it would seem to be possible to make some valid state-wide comparisons. But until recently there has been no way of adjusting for the marked variations in the difficulty of examinations from subject to subject and from year to year in the same subject. Even now, this adjustment can be made only several months after the examination. Consequently, the adjustment is probably seldom, if ever, made. National comparisons can be made through the use of standardized achievement tests, but these tests seldom correspond to specific courses, and local schools almost never use them as a basis for marking.

It may seem that marking relative to a student's own apparent ability avoids comparison with others, but the only basis a teacher has for knowing what to expect of a student is comparison with what others of comparable ability achieve. Even at that, the question of whether he is "working up to ability" is not answered, because comparable students are probably not achieving to the limit of their ability. Indeed, no norm should be considered a "satisfactory" level of attainment. A norm is merely the level, possibly quite inadequate and improvable, that happens at present to prevail.

When the course material and expectations vary for different ability sections of a grade, as they should, each version of a course should be given a distinctive title or designation. Then marks assigned on the basis of comparisons within each version will have meaning. Since each version has its own designation, it is clear that there is no relation between marks in different versions, just as there is none between those in different courses. Ungrading of the secondary school necessitates the use of "phases" or "levels" in each subject to which marks can refer, regardless of what grade students would conventionally be in.

What symbols—numbers, letters, or words—a school uses for marks is relatively unimportant. What *is* important is that the symbols communicate efficiently and unambiguously. Numbers have the advantage of being easy to manipulate. A teacher with a marking book full of letters must somehow convert them to numbers that he can average out at the end of the marking period or term.

The key question is, how many distinctions can the teacher make? When the symbols are percentages, teachers commonly try to make some forty or more distinctions, whereas other schemes limit the number to three, five, ten, or some other relatively small number. When fewer distinctions are made, less information is provided. In some subjects, two distinctions—"Pass" and "Fail" or "Satisfactory" and "Unsatisfactory"—may be all that is possible or necessary. The inclusion of a third category—"Honor," "Commendable," or "Superior"— adds a little more information.

The most common systems use five letters or numerals. When plus and minus signs are added, the number of distinctions increases to thirteen. Probably few teachers can really distinguish more than ten levels of performance.

There are three considerations in marking that some teachers find difficult to understand. First, a *score* on a particular examination is not a *mark*. Second, the marks of a class need not conform to a "normal" distribution. Third, the question of "failing" is separate from, though related to, the question of marking. Thus, three different judgments are always involved. First, the teacher must judge as to the adequacy of answers and the relative importance of questions on an examination or an assignment. The result is a score. Then he must interpret this score with reference to those of a comparison group. From this judgment a mark results. Finally, whether that mark is "passing" or "failing" is still another judgment and one that in effect recommends certain consequences. That a score is not a mark is evident from the fact that a teacher can construct an examination and a scoring system in which a given score, say 78, is the highest score of a class or the lowest. Certainly, he cannot tell automatically what mark a student with a score of 78 should have. When a teacher *scores* on the basis of 100 and also *marks* on that basis, it is all too easy for him to confuse the two and equate scores with marks.

The teacher should not expect a normal distribution of scores. It is altogether possible that the members of the class are not there purely by chance. In required courses, which are taken by all students in a grade, it is common to find a distribution with a concentration of scores near the middle and with relatively fewer toward the extremes. Not every section, however, is representative of the entire grade. Sometimes information about the relative distribution of ability in a section can serve as a rough guide to the pattern of marks that would be appropriate in that section. It would be unusual for all the members of any class to perform equally well and, consequently, to be assigned the same mark. But if the poorest performer achieved most of the objectives of the course creditably, it would be ridiculous to "fail" him merely because he was the lowest. He may even be entitled to a mark as high as "B."

Every teacher should reflect on the meaning of the word "fail." While the meaning of "failure" may be vague, its possible consequences are quite clear: the student must repeat the course if it is a required one, receive no credit whatsoever for his efforts if it is an elective, perhaps discontinue study in the subject, possibly drop out of school altogether. Judgment on passing and promoting students should be positive rather than negative. It is *not* what the student cannot or should not do that is important, but what is professionally recommended as his wisest course of action in view of his performance. The decisions are of a quite different order from the assignment of marks generally—a "B" is "almost as good as" an "A," but a "fail" is not almost as good as a "pass," no matter how close the student came to "passing." An "E," representing the lowest level of performance in a group, is not necessarily an "F," representing a "failure." Of course, school policy usually specifies the "passing" mark, but each teacher ultimately decides which students fall below it. Teachers need not fear that by giving a "D" instead of an "F" they are letting into college students who have no business going, nor should they conclude that a student who is repeating a course will necessarily learn what he failed to learn the first time.

In elementary schools pupils are promoted to the next grade on the basis of over-all performance. Often standardized test data are taken into account. In the senior high school promotion decisions are made subject by subject. Promotion in junior high school is often by subject in grade nine and by grade in grades seven and eight. Sometimes seventh- and eighth-grade subjects are classified as "major" and "minor," and a student must "pass" the "major" subjects in order to be promoted. A change to promotion by subject is long overdue in the junior high school. And throughout the secondary school a greater distinction is needed between "standards" in required courses and in courses students take for purposes of their own. Even the law cannot compel a person to do better than he is capable of doing.

INSTRUCTIONAL MATERIALS

Textbooks, which are probably the most familiar instructional materials in the secondary school today, once served to compensate for poorly prepared teachers. Excessive reliance on a textbook still suggests that a teacher is not in full command of his subject. There are exceptions to this generalization, of course. A teacher of mathematics, for example, is probably well advised to base his teaching solidly on a good textbook. But, even in this subject, instruction that begins and ends with the text is unlikely to stimulate students to discover relationships and develop generalizations for themselves. And the teaching of science exclusively from a textbook, with no opportunity for students to handle materials and explore natural phenomena, is a spiritless endeavor. In science, as in literature and history, the availability of inexpensive paperback books has opened up a rich source of instructional materials. Students of literature need no longer be limited to an anthology, and in history students can draw on original treatises and primary documents. Ironically, at a time when the quality of textbooks is improving dramatically, the need to rely on them exclusively as instructional materials has greatly diminished.

A teacher must work hard, however, to keep informed about the vast array of materials that are available. He can turn to the librarian for information and advice on many items and to the coordinator of audio-visual materials for help with others. But the teacher's best source of guidance is frequent discussion with his own departmental colleagues. In fact, all instructional materials should probably be requisitioned on a departmental basis, so that useful items will not be overlooked or needlessly duplicated.

There are four types of material about which teachers need to keep informed. One is the verbal type, such as textbooks, paperbacks, and other supplementary materials, including books for the school library and the wealth of free or inexpensive "fugitive materials," such as pamphlets, that are readily available. A second type consists of the equipment and apparatus that are widely used in science and the practical arts, and even, occasionally, in English and the foreign languages. This equipment, which is intended to facilitate some instructional task, is often redesigned, and new items appear constantly.

The third type consists of various devices for presenting information visually and aurally, including teaching machines. Many of these devices have long been familiar: projectors for slides, film-strips and motion pictures, opaque projectors, and record players. But new ones are increasingly used, such as overhead projectors (and devices for preparing transparencies for them), tape recorders, elaborate language-laboratory equipment, and film-loop projectors for showing brief single-concept motion pictures.

Fourth, and more important than the devices themselves, is the material that is used with them. A teaching machine serves merely to present an instructional program. To require students to spend time on an inferior program is as bad as subjecting them to an incompetent teacher. The same is true of films that are not relevant to the instruction or that are factually inaccurate. Annotations or advertisements for films, records, and other materials suggest to teachers items that might prove useful. But only through actual previewing can teachers make valid decisions on what materials to use with a class.

Administrators are responsible for seeing that teachers have the tools they need for effective instruction. But it is up to teachers to keep currently informed about available instructional materials, equipment, and devices. And the way to keep informed is to consult the professional journals, to examine publishers' and manufacturers' catalogs and announcements, and to attend exhibits at professional meetings. Many of the larger school systems and some colleges and universities maintain instructional materials centers at which teachers can examine sample items. In general, school boards provide too little money for equipment and supplies for the schools to obtain the maximum benefit from what is allocated for professional salaries. Many boards, of course, are quite ready to make available whatever is needed to provide the best possible instruction. If what is needed is never requested, the teachers are probably at fault.

## Suggestions for Class Discussion and Further Investigation

1. Consider whether discipline is possible without punishment. If it is, how is unacceptable behavior to be handled? If punishment is necessary, what are the characteristics of good punishment? Give examples of inappropriate punishments in secondary schools.
2. Discuss the kinds of pupil behavior that should not be tol-

erated by teachers. Attempt to identify variations in what is considered by teachers to constitute acceptable behavior.

3. Under what circumstances should teachers seek outside help with discipline problems? What kind of help should be expected from administrators? From guidance personnel or psychologists?

4. What purposes are school marks expected to serve? Can one mark serve all these purposes?

5. Discuss the meaning of "passing." What is the effect of some teachers' being "strict markers" and others' being "easy markers"? Is a difference in "standards" implied? What would be considered an "excessive" failure rate? What factors would determine how many "A's" there should be in a class?

6. Obtain and duplicate three brief selections of writing done by tenth-graders. Have a number of individuals assign numerical marks to them. Have another group mark them on the assumption that they were written by seventh-graders. Compare the marks assigned within and between the two groups of raters. Draw conclusions from the data.

## Suggestions for Further Reading

Although the most valuable insights into discipline must come from a study of the psychological literature dealing with human behavior, especially during adolescence, one booklet that many teachers have found helpful is *Discipline for Today's Children and Youth,* by Fritz Redl and George V. Sheviakov (Association for Supervision and Curriculum Development, 1956).

A discussion of marking and reporting is to be found in *Evaluating Pupil Growth,* by J. Stanley Ahmann and Marvin D. Glock (Allyn and Bacon, 1958) pp. 530–67. Further sources on marking are listed in a selected bibliography prepared by Edith S. Greer, *Pupil Marks and School Marking Systems* (U.S. Office of Education, 1963).

Some papers relating to research on various types of instructional media are presented in *Newer Educational Media* (The Pennsylvania State University, 1961). A somewhat sensational account warning of efforts to control the materials used in schools is provided by Jack Nelson and Gene Roberts, Jr., in *The Censors and the Schools* (Little, Brown, 1963).

# Chapter Ten

# Tradition and Innovation

Sometime during the decade following the Second World War, American secondary education entered a new and exciting era. A sudden increase in public interest and criticism caught educators by surprise. For years they had worked almost unnoticed and without precedents to devise a system of universal secondary education. Through boom and bust, peace and war, they had expanded curricula and adapted methods to make available and attractive to all the people's children what was formerly intended for only the few. Traditions died hard, and school patrons were not always easily convinced of the desirability of change. For the most part, however, they went along with the proposals of the educators, whose judgment they respected. Indeed, over the years the American people acquired a blind faith in education of any kind, and they took for granted the superiority of their schools.

Then, at mid-century, a constellation of factors focused public attention on the schools. Long overdue school construction required heavy capital expenditures. An increasing birth rate caused elementary-school enrollments to soar, resulting in still more construction, overcrowding, double sessions, and teacher shortages. School costs rose rapidly. Scholars and prominent figures began to write books and popular articles criticizing school programs and practices. Fear of communist subversion led to investigations of schools and textbooks. Supreme Court decisions requiring desegregation and prohibiting Bible-reading in schools centered more attention on them. Increased automation displaced workers, eliminated many lower-level occupations, and made a high-school diploma and a college degree more important than ever. Finally, Russian space successes in the midst of cold-war tensions made the American people acutely aware of the vital importance of a first-rate educational system.

Thus, demands for quality began to overshadow problems of numbers and concerns about costs. Communities prodded their schools into making changes, and the level of financial support increased. Excellence became the goal; innovation, the means. Yet, despite the sense of urgency, excellence proved difficult to define, and innovation proved difficult to achieve. Consequently, great opportunities and challenges lie ahead for secondary schools.

## THE PURSUIT OF EXCELLENCE

The call to excellence was directed not only at the schools but at the nation as a whole. Mediocrity in any field of endeavor was deplored. Observers pointed to the poor physical fitness of Americans, to the shoddy workmanship in products and services, and to the low standards of public entertainment. A federal official called television programing a "vast wasteland." A professor accused the schools of being "educational wastelands." The United States was said to lack the will to win either the Korean War or the Olympic games.

To many people excellence in the schools meant high intellectual achievement. The schools were charged with being anti-intellectual and with eliminating competition among students. Critics claimed that students were allowed to avoid difficult subjects, and studies[1] showed that adolescents valued popularity and athletic prowess more than academic achievement.

Some voices were raised, however, in behalf of balance in the school program and of excellence in all areas. Not all students can excel academically; some are artistically talented, some have special leadership qualities. Excellence can mean outstanding athletic performance or a high level of craftsmanship in woodworking. Perhaps creativity is more important than excellence, it was argued, and the intellectually gifted may not always be the most creative students.[2]

Nevertheless, many schools began to give greater emphasis to intellectual development. Special provisions were made for intellectually gifted and academically talented students. Merit scholarships were instituted, early college admission was tried, and college-level courses leading to advanced placement and credit were introduced. Science fairs and "mathletic" contests gave recognition to outstanding pupils, and accelerated programs challenged bright junior-high-school students.

A school climate in which the pursuit of excellence is encour-

1 James S. Coleman, *The Adolescent Society*, Free Press, 1961.
2 Jacob W. Getzels and Philip Jackson, *Creativity and Intelligence*, John Wiley, 1962.

aged is a stimulating one for teachers. But it is also challenging and, for some, threatening, because it demands excellence of teachers, too. A teacher whose knowledge of the subject he teaches is inadequate or outdated is the greatest barrier to excellence in a school. Not being a scholar himself, he does not value scholarship.

## THE SENSE OF URGENCY

In times of war, the secondary schools have responded to national needs by adding courses, modifying schedules, and taking on activities associated with the war effort. Only recently, however, has educational excellence become closely identified with the "national interest." The federal government has provided financial support for selected elements of the program and for particular groups of students. In the name of the national interest, schools have adopted programs to induce dropouts to return to school, have changed organizational patterns to reduce racial imbalance, and have made special provisions for culturally disadvantaged students in response to national efforts to eliminate poverty. Federally supported curriculum projects have developed new science and mathematics courses. With a sense of urgency, many schools have tried to bring programs up to date and to make instruction more rigorous.

For various reasons not all secondary schools have responded to the ferment for change. Schools are locally controlled, and a provincial view of education dominates many communities. Their criterion of adequacy embraces local needs but not the national interest. The greatest insistence on a clear priority for academic learning has been evidenced in better-educated suburban communities. In some places such priority is equated with imbalance.

The fear of imbalance is great among those teachers and administrators who were most strongly committed to the idea of the school's being responsible for promoting all aspects of students' development and preparing them for all facets of living. Thus, the most reactionary elements in the secondary schools today consist of those who consider themselves most "progressive."

Yet the urgency of redirecting the secondary schools is not due primarily to international competition but to a realistic assessment of the needs of the times. No longer do relatively few high-school graduates continue their education. No longer is early vocational training valuable. No longer are the schools serving the children of parents with little or no education. More than many realize, the times have changed and will continue to change.

Solicitous people fear the effects upon students of pressures for achievement and excellence. Recent curriculum studies suggest, however, that children can learn advanced material earlier than had been supposed. There are limits, of course, to what can be expected of students, but not until much more curriculum reform and instructional innovation have been tried will those limits even be discerned. The pressures that are most keenly felt are those operating on teachers and administrators to effect changes.

INNOVATION AND INERTIA

Modern school administrators are trained to think of themselves as "change agents." Their role is not one of maintaining the status quo but of bringing about educational improvement. This of course means change, but not innovation for the sake of innovation. It does not mean adopting every new practice that gains publicity.

If wise decisions are to be made regarding needed changes, teachers must participate in making them. Competent administrators know that it is unwise to try to impose changes on a faculty which has not been consulted about them and is not prepared to carry them out. But teachers must be willing to help identify needs for improvement, to keep abreast of innovations elsewhere, and to acquire new competences when needed. Community resistance, lack of resources, and the inertia of tradition create enough obstacles to improving secondary schools without adding an apathetic, uncooperative, or uninformed faculty.

The beginning teacher has two advantages with respect to innovation. His recent preparation enables him to note curriculum features that are not in accord with the best contemporary scholarship. One of the obstacles to modernizing the curriculum is that so many experienced teachers, especially those whose initial preparation was weak or who are teaching outside their field of specialization, are not familiar with current thought in their subjects. To overcome this problem, many colleges and universities conduct institutes in the summer and during the academic year, and national curriculum study groups provide detailed guides for teachers. But the retraining task is enormous, and new teachers should recognize the importance of keeping abreast of their fields. The teacher must first and always be a scholar.

The second advantage new teachers have is that they are not committed to traditional school practices. They are usually more willing to explore the possibilities of team teaching, to see what use can be made of programed instruction, to try new instructional media, and to consider completely new approaches with an open mind. Though they risk being resented by experienced teachers and resisted by reactionary principals, they are in an excellent position to spur innovation in their schools. Alert faculties and enlightened administrators welcome them.

The one disadvantage inexperienced teachers have is lack of experience; time, of course, rectifies this. Whether the teacher grows in competence as he gains experience depends on how self-critical he is and whether he gets the help he needs. Some need little or none, but a few need much help merely to survive, and many could be helped to become better teachers than they are. It is unfortunate when teachers find that no supervisory assistance is available to them after they have completed their preservice preparation. Larger secondary schools usually offer some kind of supervision, but many teachers begin their careers in small schools.

Providing supervision presents difficulties in any secondary school. Ostensibly the principal is the instructional leader of the school. Usually he is too busy with administrative matters to devote the time to supervision that he feels he should. Some principals never observe a teacher even once during his entire first year. Others are required by the policies of the system to make three or four or even more observations. But this requirement is usually imposed not so much to help the teacher as to assure the administration of a sound basis for personnel decisions relating to tenure and salary. Most principals are sincerely interested in helping teachers succeed and improve, but teachers are often reluctant to reveal their need for help to an administrator, whether or not his visit is required. What is more, since administrators are seldom specialists in the teacher's field, they are not always in a position to offer much help anyway.

These two factors—the teacher's willingness to seek help and the supervisor's competence to provide it—determine to a great extent the success of supervision in a school. A department head or a system-wide subject supervisor is usually technically best qualified to assist teachers with teaching techniques and instructional planning. When the proper relationship exists between them, a teacher is as likely to invite a supervisor to observe a class in which something particularly interesting is occurring as one in which the teacher has a problem. Self-critical teachers welcome reactions to their performance and suggestions for its improvement. One of the distinct advantages of team teaching is that teachers become accustomed to assessing each other's ideas and performance. A teacher can learn both from observing others and from being observed.

Supervision in secondary schools has been closely associated with in-service education and local curriculum development. In the 1940's and early 1950's many schools set up elaborate schemes for curriculum improvement. Working cooperatively with one another and with citizens' advisory groups, teachers studied the characteristics of students and the community and then tried to devise a curriculum that would serve local needs and "meet the needs of youth." Consultants from nearby colleges often served as "resource people." Much time was spent collecting data about the community and about the activities, plans, interests, and problems of students. Participation in "action research" of this kind not only served as in-service education for teachers, but resulted in curricular and instructional innovation.

Much has happened in recent years to change the situation. In the late 1950's attention shifted to the structure and content of the subjects in the curriculum. The kind of in-service education that many teachers most needed was advanced study in their teaching fields. Schools began to sponsor in-service courses and to urge teachers to attend summer institutes. At the same time, curriculum activity shifted to the national level as scholars in various disciplines undertook to devise new courses. Curriculum development requires more time and specialized knowledge than teachers usually have. Furthermore, there seems to be little reason for each community to have unique courses.

Still, each school faces the problem of overcoming inertia to get new courses introduced and to get promising innovations adopted. Somehow it must encourage its teachers to be creative in attacking problems that national groups cannot, or at least do not, attempt to solve. Most of the curriculum study in which scholars have engaged has been fragmentary; it has given little if any attention to coordination among subjects in the school program, to articulation among the various school levels, or to adaptation of courses to different ability levels among students. These are matters to which the schools must attend, and a teacher should expect to work with colleagues in his subject to devise suitable courses for all students and with teachers of other subjects and at other levels to maintain coherence and continuity in the program.

Not surprisingly, but perhaps ironically, it is the best schools that are most aware of their shortcomings and most determined to do something about them. Teaching in one of these schools is exciting. The teachers are well prepared and well informed; they engage in serious conversation, try out new ideas, undertake occasional controlled experiments, assume responsibility for the quality of the program, and vie with administrators in proposing innovations. Weak schools, where improvement is needed most, have none of these characteristics. Yet the fact that so much needs to be done can make teaching in such schools challenging instead of disheartening. The new teacher who feels a sense of urgency about getting on with the pursuit of excellence in the secondary schools can bring and promote some of the necessary characteristics. Even though he can do little to overcome the inertia of tradition and indifference, he can achieve excellence in his own teaching and he can at least initiate a dialog that might in time stimulate innovation.

## THE CONTINUING DIALOG

Talk is no substitute for action, but dialog among those who are in a position to act may clarify what needs to be done and spur someone to do it. For all the urgency of getting on with the task of improving secondary education, nothing is to be gained from precipitous change unguided by careful thought. Furthermore, many people, both professional and lay, need to be convinced that any change is needed or that change in a particular direction is desirable. Some of the views about secondary education expressed in this book represent a minority position.

The characteristic reaction of educators to criticisms of the secondary schools has been a defensive one. Weaknesses are denied, and the credentials of the critic are questioned, particularly if he has "never taught a day in a secondary school in all his life." Sometimes the very person who denies the existence of shortcomings claims they are inevitable and due to causes beyond the control of the school. Some of this defensiveness is understandable in view of the tactics of some critics who have ridiculed sincere educational leaders and have accused them of maliciousness and even conspiracy. Moreover, the spurious comparison of American schools with far less universal European systems has properly angered many educators. But their rejoinder that today's schools are better than ever is also spurious. The real questions are whether they are good enough and whether they can be made better. And if they can be improved, they are not good enough for the United States at this point in history.

The dialog has many facets. Some issues relate to societal concerns, such as desegregation, helping the disadvantaged, maintaining church-state separation, combating censorship, and solving social problems through the schools. Teachers should have reasoned views on these and similar questions. Another aspect of the dialog involves educational practices. Teachers must adopt positions on programed instruction, educational television, ability grouping, team teaching, nongrading, marking systems, interscholastic athletics, and middle-school organization. But the key question, the central issue, has to do with the instructional program of the school.

Somehow an accommodation must be reached between two fundamentally different viewpoints. The two are in agreement on one matter: they both reject the still prevalent emphasis on the acquisition of large bodies of inert facts. In its place, however, the one favors practical skills and socially useful knowledge, while the other favors intellectual skills and disciplined knowedge. There are many variants of each position, but on numerous questions this basic cleavage is evident.

Should college-bound students take as strong an academic program as possible? Or should they supplement their programs with practical courses, since they will not be able to take them in college? Can the college-bound be identified, or is it better to speak of those with college "potential" so that none will find himself ineligible when it is too late? Is an academic program of even greater importance to those who do not go to college, since high school is their last opportunity to study academic subjects? Would an academic program be best for all students if the work could be adapted to their abilities, or are practical subjects preferable anyhow?

Does the trend toward earlier and longer specialization in colleges and universities suggest that the task of providing education in the liberal arts will increasingly devolve on the high school? Should the high schools resist offering advanced courses that have in the past been identified with the colleges? Or will improved instruction and better curriculum design make higher-level achievement possible throughout the secondary school? Does the fact that each generation of parents has more education make it possible for each generation of students to achieve more in school? Will the great expansion of two-year junior and community colleges make an academic program essential for a growing proportion of high-school students?

Should vocational preparation begin as early as possible? Or should it be delayed as long as possible? Will vocational training require an increasing amount of prior academic education? As more and more students take academic programs will there be, instead of an intellectual élite, a small, alienated group that does not share the cultural and intellectual interests of the society as a whole? Are these students really incapable of grasping the key concepts of the various disciplines and of understanding how knowledge is discovered? Or are they merely unable to master large quantities of detailed and unrelated information and to acquire skills for which no rational basis is given?

Have the schools underestimated what students can learn when instruction is properly organized and skillfully conducted? Have they been overly pessimistic about the possibility of adapting the curriculum to various learning rates and overly optimistic about meeting all the nonintellectual needs of students, about changing their over-all behavior patterns, about accomplishing the total task of making good citizens and family members, and about solving social problems directly?

A continuing dialog among teachers, administrators, scholars, educationists, and laymen is essential. National concern and scholarly enthusiasm are not enough; projects, reports, and articles cannot change the schools. So long as local citizens and school boards do not demand and support change, the schools can stagnate. So long as administrators do not stimulate and facilitate change, traditional practices will persist. But all the government officials, educational leaders, interested scholars, forward-looking school boards, and alert administrators put together are powerless to improve schools if teachers lack the conviction, commitment, and competence needed to effect improvements. Fortunately, a teacher can single-handedly contribute to the betterment of secondary education merely by adding to his own knowledge and increasing his own competence. But only through the joint efforts of many people with bold vision can the American secondary schools achieve the excellence that our young people deserve and our future demands.

*Suggestions for Class Discussion and Further Investigation*

1. Examine a set of curriculum guides for elementary-school subjects. Note what science and social studies concepts and what mathematical and language facility entering seventh-graders may be expected to possess.

2. Examine the manual of the Advanced Placement Program. Note what courses are included and especially the content of courses in your own teaching field.

3. From a syllabus or curriculum guide, choose a topic in your teaching field. Then plan one adaptation of that topic for below-average students and another for academically talented students.

4. Devise a plan whereby teachers in service could be helped to recognize and overcome weaknesses in their teaching. How should administrators deal with teachers who do not voluntarily seek such help? Has the teaching profession itself a responsibility to guarantee the competence of its members?

5. If you had a grant of one million dollars, what innovation in secondary-school programs or procedures would you like to see tried?

6. Discuss in class or with colleagues some of the questions in the final section of this chapter.

7. Examine the *Evaluative Criteria* (National Study of Secondary-School Evaluation, 1960) and the *Evaluative Criteria for Junior High Schools* (1963). These are used in accrediting schools. Are the criteria forward-looking, or do they perpetuate conventional school practices?

*Suggestions for Further Reading*

John W. Gardner's *Excellence* (Harper & Row, 1961) discusses standards throughout American society and examines the conflict between excellence and equality. Other issues are raised by Ivor Kraft in an accusation of American secondary schools, "The Coming Crisis in Secondary Education," *Bulletin of the National Association of Secondary-School Principals*, 49 (February, 1965). Responses following the article indicate the extent to which opinions differ regarding the problems and the present adequacy of secondary schools.

An indication of the ideal envisioned by a professional association can be gained from two reports from the Association for Supervision and Curriculum Development: Kimball Wiles and Franklin Patterson, *The High School We Need* (ASCD, 1959), and Jean D. Grambs *et al.*, *The Junior High School We Need* (ASCD, 1961). Another publication of this organization reports on what actually occurs in an eighth-grader's day in school: *The Junior High School We Saw*, by John H. Lounsbury and Jean V. Marani (ASCD, 1964).

Two articles by a secondary-school specialist in the U.S. Office of Education attempt to clarify the issues faced by secondary education in the present period of ferment. Ovid F. Parody contrasts the current reform movements with three earlier movements in "Quality Secondary Schools of the Future," *School Life*, 47 (November, 1964), pp. 23–27. In a sequel, "Searching for Quality in Secondary Schools," *School Life*, 47 (December, 1964), pp. 24–28, the author proposes a dialog between scholars and schoolmen and outlines the opposing views that such a confrontation would have to reconcile.

Clear evidence of the national concern over educational quality and the need for research, development, and innovation is provided by the progress report of the Panel on Educational Research and Development, *Innovation and Experiment in Education* (Government Printing Office, March, 1964). Fifty recent articles dealing with current controversies in secondary education have been collected by Frederick R. Smith and R. Bruce McQuigg in *Secondary Schools Today: Readings for Educators* (Houghton Mifflin, 1965), illustrating the on-going dialog in which secondary-school teachers must join.

# Index